Advanced Grammar in Use Supplementary Exercises

with answers

Simon Haines and Mark Nettle

with Martin Hewings

CAMBRIDGE
UNIVERSITY PRESS
www.cambridge.org

CAMBRIDGE UNIVERSITY PRESS
Cambridge, New York, Melbourne, Madrid, Cape Town, Singapore, São Paulo

Cambridge University Press
The Edinburgh Building, Cambridge, CB2 8RU, UK

http://www.cambridge.org
Information on this title: www.cambridge.org/9780521788076

First published 2007

Printed in Italy by Legoprint S.p.A

A catalogue record for this publication is available from the British Library

ISBN 978 0 521 78807 6   Advanced Grammar in Use Supplementary Exercises with answers
ISBN 978 0 521 78806 9   Advanced Grammar in Use Supplementary Exercises
ISBN 978 0 521 53291 4   Advanced Grammar in Use with answers
ISBN 978 0 521 53292 1   Advanced Grammar in Use
ISBN 978 0 521 61403 0   Advanced Grammar in Use with CD Rom
ISBN 978 0 521 61402 3   Advanced Grammar in Use CD Rom
ISBN 978 0 521 61404 7   Advanced Grammar in Use CD Rom (network version)

Produced by Kamae Design, Oxford

Contents

To the student

Advanced Grammar in Use Supplementary Exercises is for advanced students who want extra practice in grammar, without help from a teacher.

There are 168 supplementary exercises. Each exercise relates to a unit or group of units in *Advanced Grammar in Use (second edition, 2005)*, and the numbers of the relevant *Advanced Grammar in Use* units are shown at the top of the page. All the answers and some short explanations are given in the Key (pages 120–135). Some exercises ask you to use your own ideas. For these, you can check the *Example answers* in the Key. You can use this book if you don't have *Advanced Grammar in Use*, but for a detailed explanation of the grammar points, you will need to refer to *Advanced Grammar in Use*.

Many of the exercises are in the form of emails, letters, conversations or short articles. You can use these as models for writing or speaking practice.

To the teacher

Advanced Grammar in Use Supplementary Exercises offers extra practice of most of the grammar points covered in *Advanced Grammar in Use (second edition, 2005)*. Much of the language is contextualised within dialogues, emails, letters and articles, encouraging students to consider meaning as well as form. The contextualised exercises can be used as models or springboards for speaking and writing practice of a freer nature.

The book is designed for students who have already worked through the exercises in *Advanced Grammar in Use* (or elsewhere) which are relevant to their needs, but who need further, or more challenging practice.

The exercises are organised in the same order as the units of *Advanced Grammar in Use*, and the numbers of the relevant *Advanced Grammar in Use* units are shown at the top of the page. The book can be used as self-study material or as a basis for further practice in class or as homework.

Thanks

The authors would like to thank Alison Sharpe for getting them in touch with each other to work on this title, and Fiona Davis for infinite editorial help and patience. And thanks to Martin Hewings for providing the original impetus. Mark would like to thank Clare for her support, and also Bruce McGowen of Bell Saffron Walden for initial intellectual stimulus. Simon would like to thank Val for her endless patience.

Photographic Acknowledgements
The publishers are grateful to the following for permission to reproduce copyright photographs and material:

(Key: l = left, c = centre, r = right, t = top, b = bottom)

Alamy Images/©Image100 for p5(t),/©Image State for p5(b),/©David Willis for p30, /©Jane Gould for p32,/©Shout for p34(t), /©David J Green for p34(b), /©James Quine for p35, /©Bob Pardue for p57, /©Alan King for p68(cl), /©Jon Arnold for p71(t), /©Maciej Wojtkowiak for p71(b), /©Oxford Picture Library for p77, /©Photofusion Picture Library for p95; Julian Barnes – *Arthur & George*, published by Jonathan Cape, book cover on p66 used by permission of The Random House Group Ltd; Bubbles Photo Library for p88; Camera Press/©James Veysey for p83(t); Catherine Cookson – *The Moth*, published by Corgi, book cover on p75 used by permission of The Random House Group Ltd; Corbis Images/©Annie Griffiths Belt for p10, /©Jose Fuste Raga/Zefa for p15(cr), /©Kevin R Morris for p26, /©Royalty Free for p40(b), /©Simon Marcus for p40(c), /©Warner Bros/ZUMA for p45, /©Royalty Free for p64, /©Hulton Deutsch Collection for p68(cr), /©Reuters for p69(r), /©Meeke/Zefa for p100; East Anglian Air Ambulance Service for p31; Empics/©PA/Andrew Parsons for p7, /©PA/John Giles for p12(t), /©AP/Darko Vojinovic for p16, /©PA/Johnny Green for p83(b); Getty Images for pp12(b), 15(l), 15(cr), 46, 65, 78, 106; Image State/©First Light for p39(cr); Lebrecht Music and Arts for p68(tr); Magnum Photos/©Henri Cartier-Bresson for p108; NASA for p99; Photolibrary/©Workbook Inc for p76; Punchstock/©Comstock for p25, /©Comstock for p39(t), /©Digital Vision for p39(cl), /©Blend Images for p39(b), /©Corbis for p40(t), /©PhotoDisc Green for p50, /©Blend Images for p60, /©PhotoDisc Green for p62(c), /©Image Source for p68(bl), /©Image Source for p73, /©Stockbyte Gold for p74, /©Comstock for p86; Redferns/Music Pictures.com/©James Emmett for p56, /©David Redfern for p69(l); Rensselaer/©Ajayan for p72; Rex Features for pp15(cl), 71(c), 117; Science Photo Library/©Christian Darkin for p62(b).

Picture Research by Hilary Luckcock.

Illustrations by Kamae Design: pp 55, 57, 70, 96; Richard Deverell pp 8, 38, 43, 90, 101, 102; Gillian Martin pp 1, 4, 9, 14, 18, 21, 28, 36, 44, 115; Roger Penwill pp 11, 24, 42, 92, 93, 103, 116, 118

The authors and publishers are grateful to the following for permission to reproduce copyright material. While every effort has been made, it has not always been possible to identify the sources of all the material used, or to trace the copyright holders. If any omissions are brought to our notice, we will be happy to include the appropriate acknowledgements on reprinting.

For the cartoon on p. 3: 'posting a letter' by Annie Lawson. Taken from the website www.cartoonstock.com. Used by kind permission; for the text on p. 7: 'The Blizzard' from the *AA Magazine*, Summer 2003. © AA. Automobile Association Limited; for the adapted text on p. 16: 'Button your lip, interview with F1 driver, Jensen Button' by Rachel Cooke. *The Observer Sport Monthly*, March 2005. Used by permission of Rachel Cooke; for the adapted text on p. 24: 'How to be sixteen' by Guy Browning. *The Guardian*, 27 November 2004. Used by permission of Guy Browning; for the text on p. 31: 'Ice man comes into the lexicon'. *The Cambridge Evening News*, 6 September 2005. Used by permission of the Cambridge Evening News; for the text on p. 32: 'Flesh-eating squirrel stalks streets of Knutsford' by Rebecca Allison, *The Guardian*, 7 November 2002, for the text on p. 116: 'Little things that we do' by David Newnham, *The Guardian*, 10 December 2005. Copyright Guardian Newspapers Limited 2002 and 2005; for the advertisement on p. 55: 'Delta fly to America', used by permission of Delta Airlines; for the advertisement on p. 55: 'Essex Libraries', used by permission of the Essex County Council; for the screenshot on p. 55: 'Windows is shutting down'. Reprinted with permission from Microsoft Corporation; for the adapted text on p. 60: 'Joined up texting' written by Professor Helen Haste, published by the Nestlé Social Research Programme 2005. Used by permission; for the front cover artwork on p. 66: *Arthur and George* by Julian Barnes. Published by Jonathan Cape. Reprinted by permission of The Random House Group Ltd; for the text on p. 72: 'Brush up on your nanotechnology. © bbc.co.uk; for the text on p. 83: 'Simon Woodroffe, entrepreneur' and 'Jeremy Thompson, Sky News War reporter'. Taken from In the Danger Zone, *Dream, The Magazine for Honda Customers*, Autumn 2004. Used by permission of River Publishing Ltd; for the adapted text on p. 92: 'Concorde' and for the adapted text on p. 103: 'Woman on bridge'. Adapted with permission of Sterling Publishing Co Inc, NY from *Lateral Thinking Puzzlers* by Paul Sloane, © 1991 by Paul Sloane; for the text on p. 103: 'The helpful detective' by Jane Reid, from *It can't be true!* Copyright © Octopus Publishing Group Limited 1983.

Advanced Grammar in Use Supplementary Exercises

with answers

Talking about the present
(present simple and present continuous)

1 Complete this conversation between two ex-colleagues who have not seen each other for some time. Use the appropriate tense - present simple or present continuous - of the verbs in brackets. In some cases, both tenses are possible.

DAVE: So, Matt, how are things with you? You (1) .... (look) very well. I (2) .... (hear) you (3) .... (do) OK for yourself.

MATT: I can't complain. I (4) .... (run) my own consultancy business. It's pretty hard work, but I (5) .... (enjoy) the challenge.

DAVE: So you (6) .... (not regret) leaving your safe job at the bank, then?

MATT: Not a bit. I (7) .... (admit) it was a bit scary to start with, but now I (8) .... (realise) it's the best move I've ever made.

DAVE: That's great! I (9) .... (just wonder) whether you (10) .... (look) for any senior staff at the moment?

MATT: Well, I could be. But you (11) .... (not want) to move do you?

DAVE: To be honest, Matt, I (12) .... (think) about it – I've been with Evergreen for nearly five years. I've got about as far as I can with them. I (13) .... (want) a new challenge.

MATT: Well, as you know, this is a specialised line of work and I (14) .... (confess), I (15) .... (have) difficulties finding the right calibre of person.

DAVE: I (16) .... (consider) applying for a job in Australia – the money's good and it would provide the challenge I (17) .... (need), but I (18) .... (not really want) to move to the other side of the world.

MATT: Well, we've worked together before Dave – I (19) .... (believe) we could do it again. I (20) .... (expect) you'd have to give Evergreen a month's notice, wouldn't you?

DAVE: Yes, probably.

MATT: Listen, Dave, I'll give this some thought over the weekend and call you back on Monday.

DAVE: That's great! I'll look forward to hearing from you.

2A Match each of these extracts from conversations (1–10) with the most appropriate speaker (a–j).

1 Flights <u>always cost / are always costing</u> a fortune during school holidays.

2 <u>I always feel / I'm always feeling</u> better after a good night's sleep.

3 <u>I expect / I'm expecting</u> again. This'll be my third!

4 <u>You always take / You're always taking</u> money from my wallet without asking.

5 <u>I feel / I'm feeling</u> much better now, thanks.

6 This weekend <u>costs / is costing</u> me a fortune – but it's worth it.

7 <u>We expect / We're expecting</u> August to be warm and sunny.

8 <u>I weigh / I'm weighing</u> 2 kilos less than I did this time last week.

9 <u>I always take / I'm always taking</u> my camera with me when I go out.

10 As you can see, <u>I weigh / I'm weighing</u> all the ingredients very carefully.

a	someone on a diet	f	a father to his son
b	a pregnant woman	g	someone planning a holiday
c	a weather forecaster	h	a TV chef
d	a keen photographer	i	an insomniac
e	someone enjoying a luxury break	j	a person returning to work after illness

2B Now choose the correct or more natural form of the verbs in the extracts above. Sometimes both forms are possible.

3 Where might you hear or read the following?

1 The keeper's pacing up and down nervously. Smith walks slowly back, pauses, then runs up and kicks the ball. The keeper goes the wrong way. It's one-nil!

2 If we watch the CCTV recording, we can see exactly what happens. Armed police surround the house – there. A plain-clothes officer knocks on the front door and stands back. Now we can see the door opening...

3
Robot submarine goes missing in North Sea

4 I was just taking my cash out of the machine, when all of a sudden two teenagers grab the cash and my card, jump into a waiting car and...

5 This man is driving along a motorway when his wife rings him on his mobile phone and says 'Are you OK?'
'Why, what's the problem?' asks the man.
'I've just heard on the radio that there's a crazy motorist driving the wrong way along the motorway you're on.'
'There isn't just one crazy motorist,' says the man. 'There are hundreds of them!'

4　Complete this story using either the present simple or present continuous form of the verbs in the box. Each verb should only be used once.

| come　continue　go　not have　notice　see　not shine　swerve　walk　wear |

A man (1) .... home along a deserted country road after being at a late-night party. The road isn't busy, so the man (2) .... in the middle of the road. There are no street lights to illuminate the road and the moon (3) .... The man (4) .... dark clothes.

Suddenly a car (5) .... down the road well over the speed limit. It (6) .... its headlights on. At the last moment the driver (7) .... the man in the road and (8) .... tó avoid him. The man hardly (9) .... the near miss and (10) .... on his way home.

How does the driver manage to see the man walking in the middle of the road?

5　Look at this cartoon strip and tell the story using the present simple and present continuous. Use the prompts given for each picture. The first picture has been done as an example.

Picture 1: Suzie / letter / post / 'Right! That's done!'
　　　　　So, this girl Suzie takes a letter to the post. She drops the letter in and says to herself, 'Right! That's done!'

Picture 2: pleased / decisive / irrevocable

Picture 3: back home / worry / right thing?

Picture 4: Paul not bad / not end the relationship / turn round / back

Picture 5: wait / two hours

Picture 6: anxious / postman / empty box / 'It's a white envelope with blue writing.'

Talking about the past

(past simple and continuous, present perfect simple and continuous, past perfect simple and continuous)

6   Choose the best forms of the verbs to complete this early morning conversation between two friends, one of whom is waiting for her exam results.

ANNA: You look pretty rough. (1) <u>Did you have / Have you had</u> any breakfast yet?

BEV: No – I'm not hungry.

ANNA: What's the matter? Are you OK?

BEV: No, I feel terrible. (2) <u>I didn't sleep / I haven't slept</u> a wink last night.

ANNA: What's the problem?

BEV: I should be getting my exam results any day now. (3) <u>I checked / I've checked</u> the post every morning this week. They must come today or tomorrow.

ANNA: Calm down – you can't do anything about it now! You'll just have to be patient.

BEV: But it's nearly three months since (4) <u>I took / I've taken</u> the exams.

ANNA: That does seem a long time.

BEV: I know, (5) <u>I never had / I've never had</u> to wait as long as this before. It's absolute torture.

ANNA: I'm sure you'll be OK. (6) <u>You revised / You've revised</u> for months before the exams.

BEV: I know, but geography and music aren't my best subjects. (7) <u>I failed / I've failed</u> every geography exam (8) <u>I ever took / I've ever taken</u>.

ANNA: Look, here's the postman! Is this what (9) <u>you've waited for / you've been waiting for</u>?

BEV: Yes – oh dear! Can you open the letter for me?

ANNA: Brilliant! (10) <u>You passed / You've passed</u> them all! Congratulations!

BEV: That's amazing! (11) <u>I really thought / I've really thought</u> I'd failed music.

7 Complete these news reports using either the past simple or present perfect form of the verbs in the box. Use passive verbs where appropriate.

admit   agree   ~~blast off~~   instruct   lift off   plead   reach   remove   send   vote   walk out

---

▼ News in brief

A An unmanned rocket carrying supplies for the International Space Station (1) ...has blasted off... from a launch site in Siberia. The spacecraft (2) .... on schedule at 17.45 this morning with food for the crew of the orbiting space station.

B Over fifty food products (3) .... from supermarket shelves. This follows a report linking a common additive with an increased risk of cancer. Government officials (4) .... store managers to stop selling the products from midday today.

C Striking staff at Edinburgh Airport (5) .... to go back to work next Monday after negotiators (6) .... a last-minute deal. The 73 staff, who (7) .... last week in a dispute over pay (8) .... to accept the deal by a majority of 68 to 5.

D A 28-year-old New York woman (9) .... stalking British tennis star Jim Denman. Jeannie Mason (10) .... guilty to three charges of making threatening phone calls to Denman. Ms Mason also (11) .... letters to Mr Denman's wife, saying she was having an affair with the tennis player.

8A Look at these examples of intentions and expectations. Match the beginnings (1–5) with appropriate endings (a–e).

1 We had intended to call in and see you on our way back, but...

2 I was expecting to hear something today, but...

3 They were thinking about coming on holiday with us, but...

4 I was thinking of changing my car next year, but...

5 I was meaning to phone you all day yesterday, but...

a ...I never got round to it – there are always so many things to do.

b ...I'll wait and see what deals are available.

c ...it was getting late and everyone was tired.

d ...the phone hasn't rung all morning.

e ...they changed their minds when they realised we preferred sightseeing to beach parties.

8B Now look at the sentences again, and decide if they refer to an expectation (*E*), a future plan (*P*) or an intention which didn't happen (*I*).

9 Use your own ideas to complete the sentences.

1 I was thinking of replacing all my old clothes with new ones, but ....

2 I was intending to tell you the whole story, but ....

3 I was expecting to find out the results of the test this week, but ....

10 Look at these short conversations. Some of the speakers use incorrect tenses. Underline and correct any errors.

a A: I don't think Pete's coming, do you?
  B: No, I don't. Let's go home. We've been waiting long enough.

b A: So you hadn't had any warning about turbulence?
  B: No, I'd looked out of the window at the time – wondering where we were.

c A: Are you all right? You look as though you've cried.
  B: I've had some bad news, but I'm OK now, thanks.
  A: Nothing too serious, I hope?
  B: My brother's been having a motorbike accident, and he's had to go to hospital.

d A: We haven't been running out of coffee again, have we?
  B: It's not surprising, we've had a lot of visitors recently.
  A: That's true, but they haven't all drunk coffee. Quite a few of them have been asking for tea.

e A: Have you played my guitar while I was out? One of the strings is broken.
  B: No, it wasn't me.

f A: How many times had you been taking your driving test before you passed?
  B: I can't remember – I think I'd tried at least three times before.

g A: Have you been a member here for a long time?
  B: Yes, I've been belonging to this club since it opened 25 years ago.
  A: That's incredible!
  B Yes, I've seen a lot of changes in that time.

h A: Why were you so upset after work yesterday?
  B: It's one of my colleagues. He'd talked about me behind my back for the last two weeks or more.

11 Complete this bad weather story using the appropriate past form of the verbs in brackets.

THE BLIZZARD

On 30th January, people in south-east England were thrilled as the first flakes of white snow (1) .... (begin) to fall. But within two hours, mass chaos (2) .... (develop). That day (3) .... (turn out) to be the second worst day for traffic on record, with motorists trapped in their cars on the M11 motorway for up to 11 hours.

Gary Barnicott (4) .... (drive) one of the first breakdown vehicles to arrive on the scene when police (5) .... (reopen) the motorway. His first priority was to deal with a vehicle stranded near one of the junctions.

'The guy (6) .... (be) in his car all night with a wife and three young children and (7) .... (be) also diabetic. He (8) .... (have) the car heater on all night and the car (9) .... (run out) of fuel and (10) .... (lose) all battery power. I (11) .... (start) his car for him, (12) .... (accompany) him to a service station and (13) .... (check) he was OK.'

Barnicott (14) .... (go) back to work, helping other drivers, many of whose cars (15) .... (break down) for quite basic reasons such as overheating or flat batteries.

'It (16) .... (take) a while to reach people because of the conditions,' he says. 'I (17) .... (stop) regularly to check if people (18) .... (need) help. I (19) .... (prepare) flasks of coffee and tea, which I (20) .... (give) to people who (21) .... (not eat or drink) anything for hours. Actually, I was pleasantly surprised because people who (22) .... (live) near to that stretch of the motorway (23) .... (come out) of their homes early to give refreshments to motorists who (24) .... (wait) in their cars all night.'

12 Read this description of how someone made the decision to change their lifestyle. Choose the correct or more natural forms of the verbs. Sometimes both options are possible.

In the end, the decision to quit my nine-to-five job in the city and take up painting (1) <u>hadn't been / wasn't</u> particularly difficult. I (2) <u>had been thinking / had thought</u> about it quite seriously for several years. For one thing, I (3) <u>got / was getting</u> more and more weary of the train journey to and from Paris every day. When (4) <u>I'd started / I started</u> the job in the mid-1990s, I'd (5) <u>really enjoyed / really been enjoying</u> getting up early, cycling to the station and reading novels on the train. But after a few years, the novelty (6) <u>had worn off / had been wearing off</u>. Then, three years ago, (7) <u>I broke / I'd broken</u> my leg in a cycling accident and (8) <u>had / was having</u> to work from home for a few weeks. Not surprisingly, I (9) <u>didn't miss / hadn't missed</u> my daily journey.

Anyway, on the Saturday before I was due to go back to work, my girlfriend and I (10) <u>decided / had decided</u> to go out for the day. It was the first time we (11) <u>went / had been</u> for a walk since the accident. After just a few minutes my leg (12) <u>hurt / was hurting</u> so much that we (13) <u>sat down / were sitting down</u> on a bench. Just in front of us a middle-aged man (14) <u>sat / was sitting</u> painting the village scene. We got into conversation with the man who, it turned out, (15) <u>had only recently given up / was only recently giving up</u> a very responsible job as a civil servant. He (16) <u>had to / had had to</u> take time off work through stress and at that point he (17) <u>decided / was deciding</u> to quit the rat race for good and turn his hobby into a full-time occupation. He (18) <u>assured / was assuring</u> us that he (19) <u>did not regret / hadn't regretted</u> his decision, and that, although he was not as well-off as he had been before, he (20) <u>lived / was living</u> a much more balanced and enjoyable life.

By the time I got home (21) <u>I decided / I had decided</u> to write my letter of resignation and I (22) <u>even finished / had even finished</u> the first chapter of the novel (23) <u>I was planning / I'd been planning</u> to write since my early twenties.

13 Write about an important decision in your life and describe the process leading up to it. Use the first sentence suggested below and incorporate some of the phrases from the box into your description.

In the end, it was actually a very easy / difficult decision to make.

I'd been thinking about... ever since the time when...
I'd been telling myself... for some time.
The situation was becoming...
I'd asked various people for their advice and they'd all...
What finally persuaded me was...

Past and present
(mixed present and past forms)

14 Look at the underlined verb tenses in this phone conversation between a mother and her daughter. Correct any errors. If the verb is correctly used, write ✓.

SARAH: Hi Mum, I'm sorry (1) <u>I hadn't phoned</u> earlier in the week, but (2) <u>I've been</u> really busy.

MOTHER: (3) <u>I'm wondering</u> if everything was OK.

SARAH: The thing is, something pretty exciting (4) <u>happened</u>. Charlie's manager (5) <u>was telling</u> him to apply for a job in Washington.

MOTHER: Washington? You mean you're moving to America?

SARAH: No, Washington near Newcastle in the north of England.

MOTHER: Oh, that's OK. But I thought you (6) <u>were starting</u> a new job at the local school next term.

SARAH: Well, that (7) <u>has been</u> the idea, but this Washington job would be perfect for Charlie. It's exactly what he (8) <u>is wanting</u> to do. (9) <u>He'd been getting</u> more and more fed up with the job (10) <u>he's doing</u> at the moment. One of his friends, an ex-colleague, who (11) <u>has moved</u> to the Washington office about a year ago, (12) <u>is thinking</u> that Charlie is exactly the kind of person (13) <u>they're looking for</u>. But the problem is that Charlie's in two minds about living in that part of the country. He (14) <u>still tries</u> to decide whether he (15) <u>wants</u> the job or not.

MOTHER: (16) <u>That's sounding</u> very interesting for Charlie, but what about you?

SARAH: I'm sure I'll find work in a school in Washington, but I'm not going to start worrying about that now because Charlie (17) <u>doesn't even fill</u> in the application form yet!

1 *didn't phone*	10
2 ✓	11
3	12
4	13
5	14
6	15
7	16
8	17
9	

15 Alison has recently left her job and retrained as a teacher. Complete this email to an ex-colleague using the appropriate forms of the verbs in brackets. You will need to use these tenses: present simple and continuous, past simple and continuous, present perfect simple and continuous, past perfect simple and continuous. Sometimes more than one answer is possible.

From: **Frayn, Alison**
Date: **17th March**
To: **John Hodges (Email)**
Subject: **hello**

Hi John

I just wanted to let you know how I (1) .... (get on) since I (2) ....
(leave) last year. Well, first of all, I (3) .... (finish) the teacher-training course
at the college last July. I must admit, I (4) .... (find) it quite hard work.
Most of the other students (5) .... (be) twenty-somethings[1] who
(6) .... (just graduate). They (7) .... (be) very good
colleagues, and they (8) .... (treat) me as a kind of elderly aunt!

Since September I (9) .... (look for) work. I (10) ....
(phone up) about seven agencies and (11) .... (reply) to more than twenty
job adverts. At the beginning of January, my husband (12) .... (find) me my
first pupil – a young Korean girl who now (13) .... (come) to the house for
lessons three times a week.

Since then I (14) .... (begin) to get responses to my phone calls and letters.
One agency (15) .... (send) me to Marseille once a week for three hours
to teach a middle-aged Frenchman. That (16) .... (work) very well as we both
(17) .... (have) the same big company background, and the business language
he (18) .... (need) is the kind of language I (19) .... (use) every
day until recently. So, as you can see, it (20) .... (all start) to happen at last.

Do phone or email to let me know how things are with you and your family.
Best wishes
Alison

[1] *twenty-something* = colloquial item for someone in his/her twenties

10

16 Complete this urban myth[1] with appropriate forms of the verbs and words in the box. You will need to use a range of past and present tenses.

| agree   never be   become   come   complain   cook   escape   phone   not return   say   start |
| actually turn up   use (×2)   warn   work (×2) |

Problems for a young chef

Did you hear about that young chef who (1) .... in a high-class restaurant in the centre of Rome?

He (2) .... there for four months when he (3) .... ill one morning just as he (4) .... his day's work. He (5) .... a very reliable worker, and when he (6) .... about burning pains in his stomach, his supervisor only reluctantly (7) .... to let him drive to the nearest hospital. The supervisor (8) .... the young man to get back as soon as possible or he would sack him.

After four hours the cook still (9) .... , so the annoyed supervisor (10) .... the hospital where the cook (11) .... he was going to find out if he (12) .... To his surprise, after a brief conversation with the casualty department at the hospital, a specialist (13) .... on the phone and asked if the cook (14) .... a microwave oven at the restaurant.

'Yes, he (15) .... the microwave every day,' replied the supervisor.

'And is it an old microwave?' asked the doctor.

'Well, yes,' said the supervisor. 'It is one of the earlier models. Why do you want to know?'

'Stop using it immediately,' said the doctor. 'Quite obviously, dangerous rays (16) .... from the microwave and (17) .... your chef's insides.'

[1]Urban myths are well-known stories that many people believe to be true, but which, in actual fact, may be greatly exaggerated or made-up.

17 Read this newspaper story and write a suitable headline for it.

....

A man has escaped serious injury in a house fire in West London. 38-year-old Ali Rashid was woken by smoke at three o'clock on Saturday morning. Mr Rashid clambered through his bathroom window as flames swept through his five-bedroom house in St John's Wood. According to the police, the fire almost certainly started in Mr Rashid's kitchen.

18 Write short news stories related to these newspaper headlines.

1

2

COMPUTER VIRUS CAUSES BUSINESS CHAOS

....
....
....

19 Write a short newspaper story based on this photograph. Explain what happened before the photograph was taken. Write a headline for your story.

....
....
....
....
....
....
....
....

Talking about the future 1

(*will*, *be going to*, present simple and continuous, future perfect and future continuous)

20 Look at these joining instructions for a conference. Match the beginnings (1–7) with the most appropriate endings (a–g).

Welcome to the tenth annual conference of the Admiral Botanical Society. We hope that you will enjoy the experience as much as participants have done in previous years. Below is some useful information – please study this carefully.

1 As soon as you arrive...
2 Hot food will be available for new arrivals on Tuesday evening...
3 Provided you have your pre-conference documentation with you, ...
4 24-hour internet access is available...
5 By the time the conference starts fully on Wednesday morning...
6 When you leave us on Saturday, ...
7 Note that refunds for food vouchers cannot be given...

a ...please return all security passes to the desk.
b ...you will be issued with passwords for internet and email use.
c ...after you leave the conference.
d ...pick up a map of the venue and your security pass at the Reception Desk in the entrance hall.
e ...unless you arrive after 10 pm.
f ...while you are with us.
g ...you will know your way around.

We hope you have a pleasant stay, and please do not hesitate to ask for any information you require at the Reception Desk.

21 Complete the following by expanding the prompts into full sentences. Use a suitable future form.

1 A: Have you heard about Abi? She's been offered the job.
   B: (wonder / she / take it.)
       I wonder if she'll take it.

2 A: Let's have a party after your exam!
   B: Yes, but (what if / really badly / I fail?)

3 A: (Their new car / seven seats.)
   B: Just as well with another baby on the way!

4 A: I don't know if you've heard, but Carrie had a minor accident on her way home last night. She drove off the road and bumped into a parked car. She's OK though.
   B: Oh dear. I expect (she / think / her job) – she's had a lot of stress at work recently.

13

5 (concert / start / 7.30.) There'll be a chance to meet the composer during the interval!

....

6 It all seems so sad. (suppose / never see her again?) How would you feel then?

....

7 Researchers have issued another warning about rising levels of ozone in the atmosphere.
   (Levels / continue / rise / another 10 to 15 years, unless drastic action / immediately.)

....

8 (you / France this summer/ as usual?) We're thinking about Spain this time.

....

9 (you / come again soon?) It's just been so lovely to see you after all this time.

....

10 John did all that work on his brother's house and then his brother went to live abroad. (He /
    wondering why / bothered.)

....

11 It's a terrible film. (She / wishing / stayed at home.)

....

22 Two students are discussing their plans for the weekend.
Fill each gap using the most natural form of the future
and the verb in brackets.

JULIE: I'm so glad the week's finished. I'm exhausted.
HENRY: Me too. I (1) ....*'m going to enjoy*......... (enjoy) this
         weekend, and make sure I forget all about college!
JULIE: What (2) .... (do) then?
HENRY: Well, I (3) .... (meet) some
         friends tonight and I expect we
         (4) .... (get) something to eat, and then go clubbing – so I
         (5) .... (need) a really long lie-in tomorrow! Then if there's enough
         time, I (6) .... (go) shopping in the new mall. How about you?
JULIE: Well, my sister and I wanted to go to a new dry ski slope that's just opened near us,
         but it looks like it (7) .... (be) cold and wet so I bet we
         (8) .... (end up) doing something else, probably staying indoors!
         What (9) .... (do) on Sunday?
HENRY: I haven't planned anything for Sunday. I probably (10) .... (not have)
         any money left by then! I (11) .... (give) you a call if you like, and we
         could go out or something.
JULIE: Oh, that's nice of you, but it's OK. I (12) .... (finish) this term's
         coursework if I can.
HENRY: Well done, you! You (13) .... (not want) to be disturbed then! Hey, look
         at the time – I'd better go. I (14) .... (be) late if I'm not careful. Have a
         good weekend and see you on Monday!
JULIE: Yeah, you too. Enjoy yourself! Bye!

23 In this email from parents to their grown-up children about a round-the-world trip, underline any future forms that are incorrect or seem unlikely. Write suitable corrections.

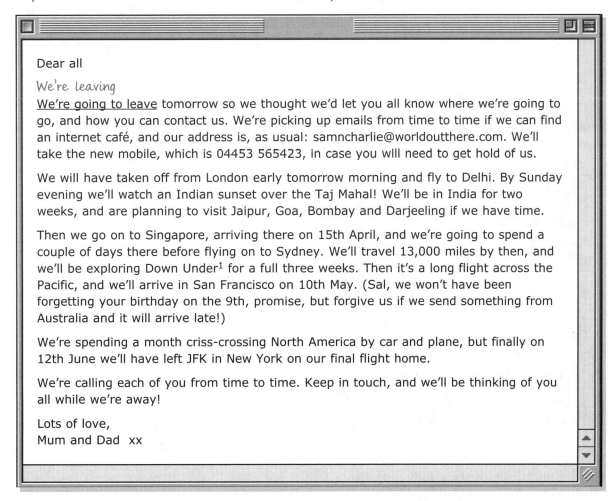

Dear all

We're leaving

<u>We're going to leave</u> tomorrow so we thought we'd let you all know where we're going to go, and how you can contact us. We're picking up emails from time to time if we can find an internet café, and our address is, as usual: samncharlie@worldoutthere.com. We'll take the new mobile, which is 04453 565423, in case you will need to get hold of us.

We will have taken off from London early tomorrow morning and fly to Delhi. By Sunday evening we'll watch an Indian sunset over the Taj Mahal! We'll be in India for two weeks, and are planning to visit Jaipur, Goa, Bombay and Darjeeling if we have time.

Then we go on to Singapore, arriving there on 15th April, and we're going to spend a couple of days there before flying on to Sydney. We'll travel 13,000 miles by then, and we'll be exploring Down Under[1] for a full three weeks. Then it's a long flight across the Pacific, and we'll arrive in San Francisco on 10th May. (Sal, we won't have been forgetting your birthday on the 9th, promise, but forgive us if we send something from Australia and it will arrive late!)

We're spending a month criss-crossing North America by car and plane, but finally on 12th June we'll have left JFK in New York on our final flight home.

We're calling each of you from time to time. Keep in touch, and we'll be thinking of you all while we're away!

Lots of love,
Mum and Dad xx

24 Imagine that you are embarking on a round-the-world trip, including these destinations: *Beijing, Moscow, New York, Paris, Rio de Janeiro, Tokyo*. Write six sentences anticipating what you'll be doing during your trip. Use suitable future forms and the time expressions in the box.

at five in the morning   this time tomorrow   by the end of next week
in a week's time   on 1st May   once in a while   when I get to

Example:
I'll have seen Paris and Rio by the end of next week!

[1] *Down Under* is a colloquial term for Australia.

Talking about the future 2
(*be to* and other future forms, future seen from the past)

25A Read these extracts from a media interview between a nervous journalist and Jenson Button, the F1 racing driver. Add the missing sentences (a–g).

In a perfect world, I would like to spend an hour, alone with Jenson Button, here in this rock-star-ish hotel in London's West End, discussing his new car. (1) .... If I am very lucky, I will get 45 minutes, but no more, and I am asked if it would be OK if his 'media liaison' woman sits in. (2) ....

I ask if I can have a few minutes alone and she agrees, reluctantly, to make herself scarce. (3) .... If Jenson could be just so kind as to turn the tape over when it runs out...

'Michael (Schumacher) is an amazing driver, and he's got an amazing team around him. (4) .... It always is. (5) .... We wouldn't be trying if it wasn't possible to beat him.'

'The Turkish Grand Prix is in August,' he says. (6) .... It's very hard to keep cool. You've got your racing kit on and then when the sun shines, it's horrible. We have about a litre of liquid, but even so.'

So what is he thinking about when he's driving? (7) .... Button looks at me as if I am stupid. 'I'm thinking about being the best driver in the world.'

a   It will be 45°C.
b   To beat Michael is going to be very difficult.
c   She'll be very quiet, they promise.
d   But no, this is not to be.
e   I really want to know.
f   But we'll try our best.
g   She will, however, be leaving behind her silver Dictaphone.

25B Which of these future forms are acceptable alternatives to a–g?

a   It is to be 45 degrees.
b   To beat Michael is sure to be very difficult.
c   She promises to be very quiet.
d   But no, this will not be possible.
e   I'm really wanting to know.
f   But we shall try our best.
g   She does, however, intend to leave behind her silver Dictaphone.

26 Here are some more extracts about sport from the media. Replace the sections in italics, choosing the most suitable future forms from those given in brackets.

1　At any moment now *the players will come out of the tunnel.* (be sure to / be about to)
　　the players are about to come out of the tunnel.

2　After another season of winning performances, *the champion is ready to take her place* in the sport's all-time hall of fame. (be set to / shall)

3　It is rumoured that *the Chelsea manager is going to leave the club very soon*, a move which will disappoint generations of fans. (be on the brink of / be due to)

4　Charles 'Skip' Walker appeared in his first international match in 1976, *but he played in 22 more* before finally retiring from the international stage in 1991. (be looking to / be to)

5　Despite his enormous success with the club, it is understood that *James Grayson plans to leave* next season so that he can devote more time to his family. (be on the verge of / intend to)

6　The ground, which has played host to international tournaments for over 75 years, *will be closed* at the end of the year. (be to / shall)

7　It is rumoured that Gaskill *is considering the possibility of a transfer* to a glamorous European club. (look to / be bound to)

8　Burton says *she will be* in the world's top 100 players by the end of this year. (aim to / propose to)

9　The organiser *has assured spectators that he will refund* ticket costs if the weather, notoriously unreliable at this time of year, prevents what has been billed as 'the race of the century' from going ahead. (guarantee to / hope to)

10　We lost the Champion's Trophy to them at the end of last season, but *we will get it back!* (be to / shall)

27A In each of these pairs of rules, decide whether the sentence is formal or informal. Mark the sentences *F* or *I*. Underline the language items which are particularly formal or informal.

1　a　Pets <u>are not to be left</u> in the buildings. (F)
　　b　You <u>shouldn't leave</u> pets in the buildings. (I)

2　a　Name cards are to be arranged in alphabetical order.
　　b　Please arrange the name cards in alphabetical order.

3　a　You know that you shouldn't carry knives, scissors or other sharp objects onto the aircraft, don't you?
　　b　Passengers shall not carry knives, scissors or other sharp objects on board the aircraft.

27B Now mark these sentences *L* for a literary style or *I* for a more informal style and underline the language items which are particularly literary or informal.

1   a We were supposed to get to the house by seven, but the snow got worse and worse and we got later and later.

    b We were to have arrived at the house by seven, but as the snow grew heavier, the journey became longer and longer.

2   a I am determined that she shall see you, whatever her doctor has decided.

    b She'll see you, whatever her doctor says.

3   a She was supposed to give him the ring, but the more she saw him, the less she liked him and in the end she didn't!

    b She was to have given him the ring, but her dislike of him grew and she did not.

28 Complete this conversation between two ex-colleagues who have not seen each other for some time. Use an appropriate future form from the box and the verb given to fill each gap.

be bound to   be on the brink of   be due to   be on the point of   be sure to   will

ANN: Is Jane here yet?

SARAH: No, but she (1) .... (arrive) any minute now.

ANN: I can't wait. She's got lots to tell us about – she's going to study in the USA!

SARAH: Really? Last time I saw her she was talking about starting a law degree in London.

ANN: Yeah, she (2) .... (fill in) the forms when she saw a programme all about studying in California, and before long she'd decided to go!

SARAH: Well, when Jane makes up her mind, you know what she's like – she (3) .... (get) to California if her heart's set on it. When is she going?

ANN: Any day now.

SARAH: It's amazing. Every time I've seen her in the last few years she seems to (4) .... (do) something exciting.

ANN: And she (5) .... (want) to know all about your plans when she gets here, so don't ask too many questions like you usually do!

29 Read this extract from an email about a weekend that held great promise, but ended in disappointment. Write a similar email about a situation where careful plans have gone wrong.

Hi Ann
Hope you had a good weekend – it can only have been better than the disastrous time I had! On Saturday morning I was going to do the shopping, but then the car broke down, so I called the emergency breakdown service. They finally arrived at 3.00, but by then I didn't have time to get any food for a picnic I was meant to be going to...

Modals and semi-modals 1
(can, could, may, might, be able to, be allowed to, will, would and used to)

30 Ed is a journalist working in a country where there are strict reporting restrictions. Read this email from Ed to his girlfriend. Think of TWO ways to fill each gap using appropriate forms of: *can, could, might, be able to* and *be allowed to*. You may need to use negative forms.

From: Burne, Ed

To: Amy

Subject: safe and well

Hi Amy

I would have got in touch sooner but I (1) _couldn't / haven't been able to_ get a signal on my mobile till now. I'm in the capital city now, so it's much easier. The other problem is, I'm not even sure whether I (2) .... use my mobile here – the authorities are very strict about certain things. I (3) .... be arrested for breaking even the most trivial law. After all the trouble I've had getting here, I (4) .... risk getting arrested or deported.

What I (5) .... tell you is that this is a fantastic country – the ordinary people are so welcoming. Not many of the adults I've met (6) .... speak any English, but some of the children know a few words. It hasn't been too much of a problem. I (7) .... communicate by using sign language and gestures.

I (8) .... tell you everything about what I've seen and done since I got here, but the highlight of my trip so far has been my visit to an ancient battlefield in the north of the country. It's an amazing place. Unfortunately, although I (9) .... take any photographs, the authorities said I (10) .... write a detailed description of what I've seen.

This is a great place, Amy. You'd love it. Perhaps if they let me come here again, I (11) .... bring you with me. I (12) .... always say you're my assistant.

Email back when you (13) .... Miss you!

Love
Ed x

---

31   Look at the underlined sections in these short dialogues. Correct any errors. If the section is correct, write ✓.

a   A: What's the matter?
     B: You, that's what's the matter. You left the oven on all night! (1) I <u>wasn't able to believe it</u> when I got up this morning. (2) <u>What had happened</u> if there'd been something inside it?

b   A: It's very quiet in here. What's been happening?
     B: Pete and Jane have been fighting again. (3) <u>The only thing I could do</u> was try to get them to talk to each other, but it didn't work.

c   A: Are you all right? What are you doing on the floor?
     B: I fell over and twisted my ankle. I tried to stand up but (4) <u>I just wasn't able to manage it</u>. I've been waiting for you to come home.
     A: I'm so sorry. I tried to phone to say I was going to be late.
     B: Yes, (5) <u>I was able to hear</u> the phone ringing – (6) <u>I just couldn't reach it</u>.

d   A: You're looking much better. How does your head feel?
     B: Pretty good thanks. (7) <u>I could go out</u> for a couple of hours earlier.
     A: Great. (8) <u>The painkillers would have helped</u>.

e   A: Oh no. I've forgotten my keys.
     B: Don't worry. (9) <u>Maggie would be at home</u> by now.
     A: No, she won't. She told me she would be late today. (10) <u>All we can do</u> is sit in the car and wait.

1   *couldn't believe it*   6   ....
2   7   ....
3   9   ....
4   9   ....
5   10   ....

32 Two friends are discussing their siblings. Decide whether *will, would, may, might, used to* or Ø (nothing) is needed to fill each gap. You may need to use negative forms.

TINA: Who were you speaking to when I came in?

SAM: Just my brother. He (1) .... keep calling me at work, and usually at an inconvenient time.

TINA: Don't you get on well with him?

SAM: We get on OK, but we (2) .... have got on better if we hadn't been so close in age. When we were children we (3) .... argue all the time. He loves arranging family reunions, but he (4) .... choose the most inappropriate places, and I find myself driving hundreds of miles to an event I don't really enjoy.

TINA: Well, you (5) .... not appreciate it now, but one day you (6) .... be glad that he's kept the family in touch, don't you think?

SAM: I suppose so. And he's very kind. He (7) .... always call or send an email if anyone in the family has a problem, and he (8) .... send me flowers from time to time when we were younger.

TINA: How lovely!

SAM: What about you, Tina? You've got a sister, haven't you? How do you get on with her?

TINA: Pretty well, actually – maybe because she's much older than me. My parents both had demanding jobs when I was little and she (9) .... look after me quite a lot. Now she (10) .... calls or drops by almost every week I should think – she lives near me. Mind you, she just (11) .... answer text messages. She says texting (12) .... stop people talking to each other.

SAM: That's a bit harsh! She (13) .... approve of me then!

33 In exercise 32, the speakers mentioned both attractive and annoying behaviour of people in their families. Think of two people you know well. How would you describe each of them?

Example:

My sister will always offer to help, and she always remembers birthdays and anniversaries. She used to be quite bossy though. When I was little she would always tell me what to do.

Modals and semi-modals 2
(can, could, may, might, be able to, be allowed to, will, would and used to)

34   Choose the correct alternatives to complete these short dialogues. Sometimes both options are possible.

a   A: Jo? Thank goodness it's you! I (1) <u>can / can't</u> tell you how good it is to hear your voice.
   B: You (2) <u>could have / may have</u> called me!
   A: I tried, but I (3) <u>can't / couldn't</u> get through. Either your mobile was switched off or you just didn't answer.

b   A: For heaven's sake, why (4) <u>won't / wouldn't</u> you tell me what the problem is?
   B: I've already told you – there isn't a problem.

c   A: I've got a really bad headache.
   B: Well, if you (5) <u>will / would</u> work late every night, what do you expect? You need to relax more.

d   A: Laura's phoned twice this morning. You should have answered the phone.
   B: I (6) <u>will / would</u> have spoken to her, but I didn't know who it was.
   A: Why don't you phone her now? She (7) <u>won't / wouldn't</u> have left work yet.

e   A: As you (8) <u>will / would</u> have read in the local newspaper, we are having to make thirty employees redundant from the end of next month.
   B: That's no surprise – I've known for a while that the company is losing money.

f   A: It's years since I've been here. The town looks completely different.
   B: It is different. For one thing, they've built a new car park where the library (9) <u>used to be / would be</u>.

g   A: Do you know whether Matt's busy this weekend?
   B: I'm not sure, I think he (10) <u>may / might</u> be going to stay with friends in Germany.

h   A: (11) <u>Are you likely to see / May you see</u> your brother today?
   B: Yes, almost certainly.
   A: (12) <u>Could / May</u> you ask him to ring me as soon as possible, please?

35 Look at these short conversations. What do you think the idiomatic expressions in italics mean?

"

1 A: He's just so untidy.
   B: Well, you know what they say: *Boys will be boys*.

2 A: No one seems to know what happened to the money.
   B: I wouldn't worry. *The truth will out*, eventually.

3 A: I've broken the window in my friend's kitchen What shall I say to her?
   B: There's not much you can say now. Unfortunately, *accidents will happen*.

4 A: What's that you're reading?
   B: It's an information leaflet for *would-be police officers*.

5 A: He's says he was feeling ill on the day of the exam.
   B: *He would say that, wouldn't he?*

"

36 Match each of these items with the phrase or sentence more likely to follow it.

1 We might go to Crete for our holiday.
2 We could go to Crete for our holiday.
a We're not sure yet.
b Would you like to?

3 You could have told me you were going to the beach.
4 You may have told me you were going to the beach.
a I can't remember.
b I'd like to have gone with you.

5 The weather might not have been very good.
6 The weather couldn't have been very good.
a You haven't got a suntan.
b However, the hotel was fantastic.

7 I think John and his family might be living in Scotland.
8 This time next year John and his family might be living in Scotland.
a It's a long time since I've heard from him.
b He's applied for a job in Edinburgh.

37   Choose the correct alternatives in this article. In some cases both options are possible.

How to be sixteen

Sixteen is one of the four ages of man that appears to be significant but isn't. The first is four – by this stage, you (1) <u>can/may</u> probably eat, talk and walk. You then realise that, despite (2) <u>being able to/being allowed to</u> do all these things, you're nowhere near being an adult.

When you get to sixteen, you (3) <u>can/may</u> cook, you (4) <u>will/would</u> have strong opinions and you (5) <u>can/may</u> well be learning to drive. You then realise that, despite being so talented, you're still no closer to being an adult.

The other two ages are thirty and sixty. Thirty is when you're meant to put aside all the things of youth and grow up – you (6) <u>may/might</u> decide to do this, but it generally takes another fifteen years. When you get to sixty, you're traditionally meant to be old, but due to the late running of previous decades, this (7) <u>can/may</u> not happen until you're in your eighties.

When you get to sixteen, it's difficult to know precisely what to celebrate, as much of the good stuff is still two years away. So it's a good idea to speak to your grandparents about what they (8) <u>used to/would</u> like about being teenagers and about what they miss from when they were sixteen. Top of their list (9) <u>could/might</u> be fully functional knees. So you (10) <u>could/may</u> want to spend an hour or two on your sixteenth birthday making use of your perfect knees. The other big thing your grandparents (11) <u>can/might</u> miss is the hearing of a sixteen-year-old. These days, just about the only thing they (12) <u>can/could</u> hear clearly is the noise of their knees creaking. Reward yourself on your birthday by using your perfect hearing. Perhaps you (13) <u>can/could</u> listen to something your parents are saying.

'Sweet sixteen' is quite a jump from 'foul fifteen'. 'Sweet' refers to the fact that life (14) <u>can/may</u> still be sweet. People (15) <u>will/would</u> soon stop asking you what you want to be when you grow up, because within a year or two it's going to be obvious. The decisions you make when you're sixteen (16) <u>may/could</u> well affect whether or not your life in the long-term will be sweet. So no pressure there then.

38   Now think about your life at different times: as a child, five years ago and now, and write two or three answers to each of these questions.

1   What can you do now that you couldn't do five years ago?

    <u>I can use spreadsheets because I've had to learn them for my job.</u>

....

2   What could you do when you were a child that you can't do now?

....

....

3   What would you like to be able to do that you can't do now?

....

....

Modals and semi-modals of obligation and necessity

(*must, have (got) to, don't have to, needn't, don't need to, should, ought to, had better, be allowed to*)

39 An opposition politician is giving a speech just before election day. Look at each underlined section of the speech and put the words in order.

I stand before you today to invite you to vote for me. We all know that (1) <u>done something must be</u> to take this country forward into a new era of fairness and equality for all, and I am the man to do it!

Let me put to you the question on everybody's lips – (2) <u>endure we must</u> another five years of incompetent government and wasteful bureaucracy? (3) <u>put up we to ought with</u> the continued misery of inflation and unemployment, issues the current government has failed to tackle? (4) <u>back stand should we</u> and let our country enter a long, slow industrial decline? Your President (5) <u>must spending be</u> his time half asleep! (6) <u>hardly remind you I need</u> that he promised an end to children living in poverty – nothing has changed!

This government, which (7) <u>have should had</u> so much energy and enthusiasm, has failed to deliver every one of its election promises! (8) <u>back I to ought stand</u> and let you vote the current government back into office?

Say no! Under my leadership, I offer you a new era, free from false hope and dark horizons. (9) <u>I need go on</u>? Vote for me tomorrow, and I will repay your trust. Thank you.

1   *something must be done* ....
2   ....
3   ....
4   ....
5   ....
6   ....
7   ....
8   ....
9   ....

40 What do you feel the priorities should be for the government of your country? Write a short paragraph. Some suggested topics are in the box.

> the arts   defence   education   environment   foreign policy
> health   taxation   tourism   trade   transport

Example:

I feel this government needs to listen to the people more – they've become rather arrogant. They should spend less time talking and more time 'doing'. They must find a way of reducing taxes, but somehow they've got to spend more on health and education. And they ought to find ways of encouraging investment in this country – we're losing too many entrepreneurs and scientists to other countries.

41 Look at this email from a colleague about a trip overseas. Choose the correct alternatives to complete the sentences. Sometimes both options are correct.

From: Clare Wootton
Date: 5th January
To: Sarah Martin
Subject: our trip

Hi Sarah

I hear you've been chosen for the trip to the conference in Cambodia! Congratulations! You (1) <u>should have been getting / must have been getting</u> yourself noticed! As I've been there before, I thought you might like some advice. (2) I <u>should've / must've</u> contacted you earlier but I've been so busy – you know how it is.

Anyway, I (3) <u>shall / should</u> get to the check-in desk as early as possible if I were you, because there are *always* queues for the night flight. I expect you'll get your currency before you go, but fortunately if (4) <u>you've to go / you've got to go</u> to the bank while you're there, you (5) <u>mustn't / don't need to</u> produce three forms of identity like you used to. I think it's still the case that any foreign currency you take in (6) <u>has to be taken out / must be taken out</u> again at the end of the trip. (7) I <u>wouldn't / oughtn't to</u> hang around at the airport – get a licensed taxi from the desk inside the terminal building and then you (8) <u>don't need to / needn't</u> worry about being overcharged. Once you reach the conference you (9) <u>needn't / need hardly to</u> worry about a thing – your hosts will make you feel entirely at home. (10) <u>You must make sure / you've got to make sure</u> you meet Jackie Els – she knows all about you.

By the way, who (11) <u>need I / should I</u> contact about the publishing project if I can't get hold of you while you're away?

I'm sure you'll really enjoy yourself. We (12) <u>would / must</u> get together when you're back and compare notes! Have a great trip!

Best wishes
Clare

42　Complete these short dialogues using suitable forms of the modals and semi-modals in the box, plus the verbs given.

> had better　have to　have got to　must　need

a　A: Does Simon (1) .... (play) that music so loudly? I'm trying to study.

　　B: He's not even here. The phone rang and he (2) .... (go out) in a hurry.

　　A: Well, in that case, I'll switch it off myself!

b　A: That's a really nice car you rented. When (3) .... (give) it back?

　　B: Tomorrow, but I've enjoyed driving it so much I might do the same again next time we have a weekend away. It (4) .... (cost) much if you book on the Internet – this one was only €100!

　　A: Really? That (5) .... (be) the deal of the year – fantastic!

c　FATHER:　Dan's been out for nearly four hours now – he (6) .... (have) a good time with his friends.

　　SISTER:　I'm worried about him. I think we (7) .... (go out) and look for him.

　　FATHER:　Don't be silly – he'll be fine. Anyway, he'll come home soon – he (8) .... (be) getting hungry!

43　Write a negative response for B using *need* in an appropriate form (*don't need to, needn't, didn't need to, needn't have*) and the verb in brackets.

"

1　A: I'm so nervous about meeting your parents.

　　B: (worry) *You needn't worry. They're really friendly and they can't wait to meet you.*

2　A: I'll wash the car before we put it in the garage.

　　B: (bother) ....

3　A: I've forgotten my mobile and I need to make a call. I'd better go back and get it.

　　B: (do) ....

4　A: I feel a little overdressed. I thought everyone would be in smart clothes.

　　B: (wear) ....

5　A: I'm really scared. This diving board looks much too high.

　　B: (be afraid) ....

6　A: I thought your sister was going to be really angry when she found out we'd broken her MP3 player, but she was really nice about it.

　　B: (worry) ....

7　A: You're early. Didn't you go to the shops on the way home?

　　B: (get) ....

"

27

44 Complete this conversation between two flatmates using the correct form of an appropriate linking verb to fill each gap. Choose from: *appear, be, become, get, go, keep, look, seem, sound.*

SAM: You (1) .... really worried. Is everything all right?

JULIA: I think so, but I was on the phone to my sister Fran, when it just suddenly
(2) .... dead.

SAM: You should try phoning her back.

JULIA: I did, but there (3) .... to be a signal.

SAM: Were you talking about anything important?

JULIA: Well, quite important. She (4) .... married next weekend, and I think she
(5) .... stressed out about all the things she's got to do.

SAM: She (6) .... cold feet, is she?

JULIA: No, but thinking about everything (7) .... her awake most of last night.

SAM: That (8) .... completely normal for someone a week before their
wedding. I was exactly the same before my wedding.

JULIA: Really?

SAM: Yeah, then two days before the big day, my boyfriend (9) .... missing.

JULIA: So what did you do?

SAM: Just hoped and prayed he'd show up. And he did. It happens quite often apparently. In fact
it (10) .... to be quite a common thing.

45 Choose the correct verbs or forms of the verb to complete these short conversations. Sometimes both options are possible.

a   DOCTOR: I'm going to prescribe antibiotics for you.
    PATIENT: Is it serious?
    DOCTOR: Not really, but your finger has (1) <u>become / gone</u> infected and we need to treat it.

b   A: I've just opened the fridge and it smells terrible.
    B: Oh no, that fish we bought last week must have (2) <u>become / gone</u> off.

c   A: What's that dog doing in my garden?
    B: He appears (3) <u>burying / to be burying</u> something. Whatever he's doing, he (4) <u>seems to be /
        seems</u> completely absorbed in it.

d   A: I bumped into your son yesterday. I hardly recognised him.
    B: I know what you mean – he (5) <u>appears / looks</u> very grown-up, doesn't he?
    A: Yes, he's (6) <u>gone / turned</u> into a very pleasant young man.

e   A: I'm going to have to take my computer back to the shop again.
    B: Why? What's the problem?
    A: It's (7) <u>become / gone</u> wrong yet again. I just don't believe it.

f   A: I had an email from Caroline yesterday. You won't believe it – since I last saw her, she's
        (8) <u>become / got</u> divorced.
    B: Not again!

g   A: Do you know what Juan's doing these days? I've lost touch with him since we left school.
    B: Yes, I do actually. He went to university and then (9) <u>became / turned out</u> a teacher.

h   A: I feel really cheated. The description in the brochure made the hotel (10) <u>look / sound</u> so
        luxurious – and the photo made it (11) <u>look / appear</u> so modern.
    B: So what was it actually like?
    A: It (12) <u>ended up / turned out</u> to be a real disappointment.

i   A: Be careful – you nearly went off the road then!
    B: Sorry, but I'm finding it really hard to (13) <u>be / stay</u> awake
    A: Do you want me to drive?
    B: No, I'll be OK, but you could talk to me to (14) <u>keep / remain</u> me awake.

j   A: Rosy and Martin are going through a bad patch at the moment, aren't they?
    B: Yes – it's (15) <u>becoming / getting</u> more and more obvious.
    A: Actually, Rosy's (16) <u>becoming / getting</u> more and more suspicious of Martin's behaviour –
        apparently he comes home late every night.

46   Read these extracts from an interview with someone who has returned to their home town after living abroad for nearly twenty years.

> I've only been back a couple of days and already I've met lots of old friends. They don't appear to have changed very much – they're as friendly as ever. And they say that I look the same as I always did. Funnily enough, hardly anyone seems to be aware that I've been away.

> How have I changed since I've been away? Well, for a start I've become more tolerant of other people and their ideas – and during the short time I've spent here in my home town, I've come to value the feeling of belonging to a particular place.

> As far as the place itself is concerned, it definitely appears to be a more prosperous, lively place than it was when I left.

Now think about changes you have experienced in recent years. Complete these sentences with ideas of your own.

1   Many of my friends seem ....

....

2   Hardly anybody I know appears ....

....

3   As I get older, I'm getting more / less ....

....

4   The town has definitely become ....

....

5   Recently, I've come to realise ....

....

47A Read this article about a life-saving idea connected with mobile phones. Complete the text with the correct passive clauses.

a the acronym is so widely used
b I was surprised by how
c if an emergency contact was stored
d I've been called to
e people are encouraged to add
f the phrase has been listed
g might even be revealed
h they'd want them to be contacted
i ~~was officially recognised~~
j would like to be contacted

Cambridge Evening News

06 September 2005

ICE man comes into the lexicon

A CAMBRIDGESHIRE paramedic who developed a life-saving idea which has taken the country by storm has been celebrating after his acronym (1) .was officially recognised. **in the English language.**

Cambridge-based Bob Brotchie, 41, came up with the idea for an ICE number, standing for 'In Case of Emergency', believing it would help (2) .... on people's mobile phones.

N-ice idea: Bob Brotchie

Now, as (3) .... , a well-known English dictionary has provided a definition and (4) .... under the new words section on its website.

Under the initiative, (5) .... the entry 'ICE' to their mobile phone address book and next to the entry list the name and number of the person they (6) .... in an emergency.

Mr Brotchie, from Mildenhall, said about the ICE initiative: 'I was reflecting on some of the accidents at the roadside (7) ...., where I had to look through the mobile phone contacts struggling for information on a shocked or injured person.

It's difficult to know who to call. Someone might have 'Mum' in their phone book but that doesn't mean (8) .... in an emergency.

Almost everyone carries a mobile phone now, and with ICE we know immediately who to contact and what number to ring. Their medical history (9) ....

(10) .... quickly the idea was adopted, but delighted to have come up with a potential life-saver.'

47B Now look at these examples of the passive from the above text, and compare them to active equivalents. Why do you think the passive was chosen in each case?

1   ...it would help if an emergency contact was stored on people's mobile phones.
    ...it would help if people stored an emergency contact on their mobile phones.
    Using the passive lets you put new or important information first.

2   ...people are encouraged to add the entry 'ICE' to their mobile phone address book...
    ...somebody encourages people to add the entry 'ICE' to their mobile phone address book...

3   Now, as the acronym is so widely used...
    Now, as people use the acronym so widely...

4   Their medical history might even be revealed.
    Being able to call the ICE number might even reveal their medical history.

5   I was surprised by how quickly the idea was adopted.
    How quickly the idea was adopted surprised me.

48 Read this news story about an animal behaving unusually. Decide whether to use an active or passive form of the verb in brackets to fill each gap.

Flesh-eating squirrel stalks streets of Knutsford

Householders in Knutsford, Cheshire, (1) ....
(disturb) by the unlikeliest of foes – a vicious grey squirrel with a taste for human flesh.

The rogue animal (2) .... (believe) to have attacked at least six residents in the past week, and his behaviour (3) .... (describe) by residents as 'well beyond a joke'.

One woman (4) .... (suffer) a nasty bite on the ankle before she could shake the tiny creature off her leg. And a two-year-old girl (5) .... (take) by surprise when the squirrel (6) .... (jump) at her, clung on to her head and (7) .... (bite) her on the eyebrow.

One resident, Blanche Kelly, (8) .... (describe / chase) round the garden by the squirrel. She admitted she would stay indoors if the squirrel (9) .... (see) near the house. 'Everyone round here (10) .... (live) in fear and they will not let their children out any more because of this violent squirrel.'

There (11) .... (think / be) very few urban squirrels which act so aggressively towards humans. It (12) .... (not yet / establish) whether the animal was originally a pet which escaped. If squirrels (13) .... (tame) when young but then let go, they can end up being rather antagonistic towards humans.

49 You have been given some notes about the highlights of a college academic year. Use the notes to write a college newsletter using passive verbs where possible.

October	Government inspectors excellent report, awarded five-star status
December	Local council vote, 'Best Educational Establishment' in area
December	Department of Education rating: one of top 25 colleges in country
March	Local company offer two top managers to teach Advanced Business Students before summer exams
May	Mention by Minister of Education as example of excellence. Teaching methods / exam results 'outstanding'
May	Request from twin college in France to send ten students to award ceremony
June	Appointment of Hilary Edwards as new Principal from September
July	Invitation to send five students to International Student Congress, New York

Hightown College Year Highlights

Hightown College has had another outstanding year. Here are just a few of the highlights.

Example:
In October, we were given an excellent report by government inspectors, and we were awarded five-star status.

50A Look at the four items from an internet news site in exercise 50B. Choose a suitable group of verbs (1–4) for each text.

1 emerge   find   treat   punish   re-inspect   threaten   see

3 report   see   observe   arrive   estimate   believe   target

2 confirm   reveal   stress   reflect   report   say   refuse

4 destroy   think   start   soak   extinguish   call back   re-ignite

50B Now use the verb sets from exercise 50A to complete each text. Use appropriate active or passive forms. You may require the form: *it + passive verb + that.*

NEWS

A

Political announcement 'completely unexpected'

In the most unexpected announcement seen for over 50 years, (1) ....
that the government will dissolve parliament and hold an election in May next year.
(2) .... also .... , completely unexpectedly, that the
Prime Minister will be standing down as party leader at the same time. (3) ....
that the announcement in no way (4) .... a lack of confidence in this
government's appetite for leadership; on the contrary, (5) .... that inflation
had fallen for the tenth successive month. Experienced political commentators
(6) .... to be as surprised as anyone, and one expert we approached,
unusually, (7) .... the opportunity of an interview.

B

Blaze that wouldn't go out

A spectacular blaze, in which, thankfully, no one was hurt,
(1) .... a factory in Wickenham.
The fire (2) .... to (3) .... by
youths who used old rags which (4) .... in petrol.
Fire officers (5) .... the blaze, but
(6) .... to the scene two hours later when parts of
the building (7) ....

C

Harsh discipline threatens school survival

Shocking reports (1) .... following the inspection of a private school in
Wallingford. The school, St Earl's, (2) .... to be using old-fashioned forms
of strict discipline. Children (3) .... harshly, and teachers routinely talked
down to them and (4) .... them without explanation. The school will
(5) .... in 3 months' time, and (6) .... with closure
unless practices (7) .... to have changed dramatically.

D

South Street break-in ... again

A theft (1) .... from a jewellers in South Street.
Just after midnight last night a figure (2) ....
breaking the window of the shop, and within moments
(3) .... leaving the premises clutching a large
bag. Police (4) .... too late to carry out an arrest.
(5) .... that the jewellery stolen was worth over
£100,000, and (6) .... that this was the fourth
time that a shop in South Street (7) .... this
year alone.

Questions

(*wh*-questions, negative and echo questions, questions with *that*-clauses)

51 Match the questions and answers from the interview. Complete the questions by adding the correct question words and phrases from the box. You will need to use some more than once.

How / How about / How often / How many / What / When / Where / Which / Who / Why

Oliver Lockman has played the trumpet in a jazz band for over twenty years. Last year he released his first solo CD which has just been nominated for a prestigious international music award. Suddenly Oliver has become public property. Everyone, it seems, wants to know all about him. Here are his answers to a set of interview questions put to him by a music journalist.

1 ....*What*....... is your idea of perfect happiness? ...g...
2 .... living person do you most admire? ....
3 And .... do you despise? ....
4 .... does your group play these days? ....
5 .... do you enjoy playing most? ....
6 .... large concert halls? ....
7 .... did you start playing? ....
8 .... different bands have you played in? ....
9 .... did you decide to bring out a solo CD after so long? ....
10 .... surprised were you to be nominated for this fantastic award? ....
11 .... has bought the CD? Have you any idea? ....
12 OK, and finally .... would you like to be remembered? ....

a Several thousand people who liked what they heard on TV, I guess!
b There were one or two of my own compositions I wanted to record and bring to a wider audience.
c Small, friendly clubs.
d I got my first trumpet when I was nine years old.
e Usually two or three times a week – more if we're on tour.
f No, I'm not keen – I prefer to keep things small.
g Playing saxophone with my band.
h Nobody – except perhaps my maths teacher when I was at school. He certainly didn't like me very much!
i Hmm, that's a tough one. Regular bands, four or five, I suppose.
j I was astonished. I'd had modest success in the past, but nothing like this.
k That'd have to be Miles Davis.
l As a nice guy who could play the trumpet a bit, I guess.

52 Complete this conversation between a mother and her teenage daughter. Use the words given to make appropriate questions.

LORNA: I'm going out now, Mum. Bye.

MOTHER: Bye, darling. Where are you going?

LORNA: Only into town – I'll be home about midnight.

MOTHER: (You'll / when) (1) .... *You'll be home when?* ....

LORNA: About midnight – I'll be OK. We're going to the Dungeon Club.

MOTHER: (You / where?) (2) .... ?

LORNA: The Dungeon Club, you know! It's not as bad as it sounds.

MOTHER: But it's miles away. How are you going to get home?

LORNA: I expect we'll walk.

MOTHER: (Would / good idea / taxi) (3) .... ?

LORNA: Mum, taxis are really expensive!

MOTHER: But you had your pocket money yesterday.

LORNA: I know, but I've spent it.

MOTHER: (You / do / what?) (4) .... ?

LORNA: Spent it – on CDs and make-up, you know.

MOTHER: (Why / never / save?) (5) .... ?

LORNA: Well, I don't get very much. Most of my friends get about a hundred pounds a week.

MOTHER: (They / how much?) (6) .... ?

LORNA: A hundred. It's not that much these days you know.

MOTHER: If you need more money, (why / part-time job?) (7) .... ?

LORNA: I don't think there are any part-time jobs around.

MOTHER: (Why / look in the newspaper?) (8) .... ?

LORNA: I could do I suppose, but I'm usually too busy.

MOTHER: (You / what?) (9) .... ?

LORNA: Busy. You know 'busy' as in having too much to do.

MOTHER: You should try getting up a bit earlier in the morning.

53 Write appropriate questions or exclamations to complete these short conversations. Use the words and phrases in brackets to help you.

"

1 A: .... ! (weather)
 B: It certainly has! The rain last night was absolutely appalling!

2 A: .... ? (accident in the car)
 B: I was going to, but I thought you'd be angry.

3 A: .... ? (MP3 player)
 B: It's Sophie's – she bought it yesterday.

4 A: .... ? (interview)
 B: It wasn't bad, but I don't think they'll give me the job.

5 A: .... ? (ring at this time of night)
 B: I don't know – shall we answer it?

6 A: .... ! (fantastic time)
 B: Yes, great! I don't normally like zoos, but I really enjoyed going yesterday.

7 A: .... ? (we / miss our flight)
 B: I suppose we'll just have to hang around and catch the next one.

8 A: .... ? (on the phone when I came in)
 B: It was only my mother – she wants to know when we're next going round to see her.

9 A: .... ? (car / bomb discovered under)
 B: The President's – that's the third assassination attempt this year.

10 A: .... ? (contestants / win the competition)
 B: Amazingly, the one who'd come last in the rehearsals.

"

54 Fill the gaps in this newspaper article about a fraud case. Use each verb given with an appropriate preposition or object.

SWIFT DECISION IN FRAUD TRIAL

Brussels, Thursday

Many observers (1) _associate_ fraud cases _with_ (associate) long drawn-out court proceedings. But late yesterday, the case of a mother-of-two bank clerk that has gripped the city of Brussels came to a rapid end, after only a day of summing up. Marie-Josephine Van Zuylen stood silently in the dock as the defending and prosecuting lawyers made their cases.

The defending lawyer said the police had clearly (2) .... (mistake) for the true criminal, and that he (3) .... (believe) innocent of the alleged crime. He (4) .... this statement .... (base) the evidence of financial transactions that had taken place when she could not have been in the building.

The prosecution (5) .... (considered) unfit to take care of the public's money, and said that her personal circumstances should not (6) ....

.... (detract) the seriousness of her actions. A series of minor crimes had (7) .... (culminate) the illegal transfer of thousands of Euros.

Summing up, the judge announced his verdict to a packed courthouse. He (8) .... (declare) satisfied that she was guilty, and barely paused before proceeding to sentence her to ten years in jail. He (9) .... (refuse) bail, but (10) .... (permit) the right to appeal. After (11) .... the court .... (remind) the gravity of the crime, he (12) .... (pronounce) closed. Van Zuylen was led away, still in silence.

Many observers afterwards (13) .... (judge) unfair, and commented that the courts had (14) .... a heavy sentence .... (inflict) an apparently innocent woman.

55 Imagine you work in the marketing department of a large supermarket chain and are responsible for writing a newsletter for regular customers. Your boss has some suggestions of how to improve a draft newsletter you have written. Make the amendments as suggested. You may need to change some of the verbs.

Look at the changes we've been making ...

We have continued our loyalty bonus card programme. Fine!

20 new stores have opened. *Begin this sentence with 'we' ...*

Our product ranges have varied. *use 'we'*

Our costs have fallen, and our prices have decreased. *use 'we' again*

We have moved newspapers and magazines to the front of our stores.

We have created new products.

TiSONS – brighter, bigger, better

1 We have opened 20 new stores.
2 We ....
3 We ....
4 Newspapers and magazines ....
5 New products ....

56 Look at these extracts from interviews with different writers. Fill each gap with the appropriate form of a verb from box A and a preposition from box B. You can use each preposition more than once.

| A | aspire ~~attribute~~ base belong culminate |
| | deal differentiate explain point out regard |

| B | as between in on |
| | to with |

'I (1) ....*attribute*.......... my success ....*to*.............. my willingness to face up to the darker side of life in my writing. I always try to (2) .... good, evil and ignorance. I wouldn't claim to be terribly original, and I (3) .... a lot of my ideas .... classical tragic literature, as a matter of fact.'

'Friends like to (4) .... me that I am an old-fashioned writer. I work at an old desk which (5) .... my father, and I sometimes even write whole chapters by hand!'

'I (6) .... most culture these days .... pretty weak – you know, TV programmes that just show you 24-hour coverage of people (7) .... everyday problems. Can anyone (8) .... me why an intelligent and free-thinking public want to watch that kind of thing?'

'While I've been pleased with my success this far, I've always (9) .... writing a series of novels, you know, a trilogy or something. Yes, I do like the idea that my writing career might (10) .... something epic like that, I really do.'

57 A teacher of very young children is ill, and has left instructions for another teacher who will be looking after her class. Choose the correct forms. Sometimes both may be possible.

N P S

Newton Primary School

Thanks ever so much for helping out. Here are a few notes that might help:

- You need to (1) <u>ask the children for their homework</u> / <u>ask the children their homework</u> before the lessons begin.

- All the records and paperwork live on the red trolley at the back of the room – get them to (2) <u>pass the register to you</u> / <u>pass you the register</u>.

- In the craft half hour, (3) <u>make models with clay for the children</u> / <u>make for the children models with clay</u> to take home. (4) <u>Demonstrate them this</u> / <u>Demonstrate this to them</u> if necessary.

- They might be shy in the music lesson, so (5) <u>sing the song to them</u> / <u>sing the song for them</u> before you (6) <u>ask to them to sing</u> / <u>ask them to sing</u>.

- (7) <u>Read a story to the children</u> / <u>Read the children a story</u> at the end of the afternoon. (8) <u>Describe the characters to them</u> / <u>Describe them the characters</u> before you start and try and get them interested.

- (9) <u>Choose a suitable book to each child</u> / <u>Choose a suitable book for each child</u> to take home from the shelves at the back of the classroom.

- (10) <u>Leave the lesson record to me</u> / <u>Leave the lesson record for me</u> and write me a note if there are any problems I should know about.

---

58 Complete this news story using appropriate forms of the verbs in the box. Add prepositions where necessary.

| be   do   get away with   impersonate   obtain   pass   stand in for   take   ~~use~~ |

Professional lorry driver took tests for learners

A former lorry driver who confessed (1) ....to using.... his skills behind the wheel to pass tests for dozens of learner motorists was jailed for six months yesterday.

Charlie Harris offered (2) .... his clients during their driving examinations in exchange for £500.

In a scam described by a judge as 'astonishing', he booked 123 theory tests and 95 driving tests for learner drivers who had given up hope (3) ....

Despite looking nothing like the photographs in the licences he produced, he managed (4) .... his deceit for months before eventually being caught out by a suspicious examiner.

Before the introduction of licences with photos, Harris would sit a theory test pretending

(5) .... his customer and, after passing, then had the documents he needed to take the practical test.

When photo licences were introduced, he simply took his chances, but limited himself (6) .... men who were about the same age as he was.

Finally, a senior driving examiner became suspicious. He visited three test centres and watched Harris (7) .... the tests. The fraudster was arrested soon after.

He admitted (8) .... six theory certificates and sixteen practical test certificates. The judge said he couldn't understand why there was nothing in the system to prevent people like Harris (9) .... this.

59 Write sentences summarising these short conversations using the verbs in brackets to help you.

A ANNA: I know we're short of money, but why did you have to do something so extreme?

   HARRIS: I didn't take the driving tests, honestly!

   ANNA: I tried so hard to stop you.

   HARRIS: I'm not going to say I did something I didn't do.

1 (resort to)   *Anna couldn't understand why he had resorted to doing something so extreme.*
2 (deny)   Harris ....
3 (discourage)   Anna ....
4 (own up to)   Harris ....

B DAVE: You convinced me to let you take the test for me.

   HARRIS: But you didn't disagree.

   DAVE: I really wanted to pass the test. At any cost.

5 (persuade)   Harris ....
6 (object to)   Dave ....
7 (admit)   Dave ....

C JUDGE: Charles Harris, by your reckless actions you have endangered the lives of thousands of
motorists. I am sentencing you to six months in prison as an example to others who
may wish to copy your actions. Let us hope that nothing like this ever happens again.

8   (accuse) The judge ....

9   (deter) The judge sentenced Harris to six months in prison in order to ....

....

10 (prevent) The judge hoped that the sentence ....

60 Read this text about someone applying for a job in the USA. Rewrite the underlined sections
using the verbs in brackets.

Last year I saw an advert for a brilliant job in the USA. The money was
good and the job would have suited me perfectly. There was only one
problem: (1) I was too frightened to tell my parents that I'd applied for a
job in the USA. (2) I knew they wouldn't want me to work abroad. Like
most parents, mine tend to worry about my safety, but they're not that
bad. (3) They have always allowed me to make my own decisions.

When I heard I'd got an interview for the job, I didn't know what to do.
(4) I even thought: 'Perhaps I won't turn up for the interview'. However, I
felt I should go since (5) the American company had made arrangements
to hold the interviews in London.

So I went for the interview and was actually offered the job.
Unfortunately, it wasn't quite as good a deal as it had sounded in the
original advert – so I turned it down. (6) In the end it was my choice not
to work in the USA.

1 (dare) *I didn't dare (to) tell my parents that I'd applied for a job in the USA.*

2 (disapprove of) ....

3 (let) ....

4 (consider) ....

5 (arrange) ....

6 (decide) ....

61 Complete this courtroom conversation between a female lawyer and witness, using either the bare infinitive or the *-ing* form of the verbs in brackets.

LAWYER: Tell the court, Ms Prochak, why you looked out of your window at 5.30 in the morning.

MS PROCHAK: Well, I had woken up because I heard someone (1) .... (try) to start their car.

LAWYER: So when you looked out of the window, what did you see?

MS PROCHAK: I saw my neighbour, the defendant, (2) .... (hit) the steering wheel of his car and (3) .... (shout) angrily.

LAWYER: Can you be more precise, Ms Prochak? Did you observe your neighbour (4) .... (strike) the steering wheel once or several times?

MS PROCHAK: I saw him (5) .... (punch) it continuously.

LAWYER: And did you actually hear him (6) .... (shout)?

MS PROCHAK: No, but I knew he was because I could see his mouth (7) .... and .... (open and close).

LAWYER: I see. And what happened next?

MS PROCHAK: I saw him (8) .... (get out) of the car, (9) .... (slam) the door and (10) .... (walk) away.

LAWYER: And can you tell the court what happened the next time you saw your neighbour?

MS PROCHAK: Yes, the next time I saw him was about ten minutes later, when I happened to look out of the window again. I saw him (11) .... (pour) petrol over his car. I ran to phone the police – but as I was describing what I had seen I heard the car (12) .... (explode).

62 Write sentences describing things you have seen or heard recently. Write about real or imaginary experiences using these verbs: *feel, notice, overhear, see, watch.*

1 As I was walking home the other night, *I noticed someone trying to break into a car.*

2 On the train the other day, ...

3 While we were driving along the motorway recently, ...

4 On our visit to the wildlife park, ...

5 As I walked through the crowds of people, ...

63 Sanjeev is asking about his friend Henry's appearance on a radio quiz. Fill the gaps using the original words of the quiz presenter to help you.

SANJEEV: I'm so sorry I missed your moment of fame! So, how did it go? How did they start?

HENRY: Pretty good! At the beginning they (1) <u>warned me I would have</u> just 10 seconds to answer each question, but (2) .... me nervous.

SANJEEV: Yes, and what questions did they ask?

HENRY: The first one was (3) .... ! But then they started the real questions. They (4) .... – I got that right, Kathmandu – and they (5) .... tea growing. I said India and Sri Lanka, so that was OK.

SANJEEV: Great! And then?

HENRY: It got more difficult then, because they started asking about sport. They (6) .... of the 2002 European Cup, and I just couldn't remember, and they (7) .... for three years in the 70s – that was far too difficult!

SANJEEV: Oh dear. After that?

HENRY: It got better again at the end. They (8) .... 5 million, 15 million or 150 million kilometres from the earth, and I guessed 150. Finally they (9) .... the current US Vice President. And that was it!

1 Remember, you've only got 10 seconds to answer each question!

2 We won't make you nervous, we promise!

3 Is your partner listening?

4 What's the capital of Nepal called?

5 Do you know two countries where you can find tea growing?

6 We'd like to know the winner of the 2002 European Cup.

7 Why didn't Muhammad Ali box for three years in the 1970s?

8 Is the sun 5, 15 or 150 million kilometres from the earth?

9 I wonder if you can name the current US Vice President?

64 Here is an interview with film director Tim Burton about his film *Charlie and the Chocolate Factory*. Report each underlined section using a verb from the box. You may need to add an additional clause.

add   admit   agree   believe   disagree   explain   stress   suggest

| **Tim Burton** | Interviewed by Anwar Brett |

Since his breakthrough film *Beetlejuice*, director Tim Burton has brought a distinctly macabre touch to a succession of movies, from *Batman* to *The Nightmare Before Christmas*. He's now brought Roald Dahl's *Charlie And The Chocolate Factory* back to the big screen. He had a son, Billy Ray, with partner Helena Bonham Carter in 2003.

You shot *Charlie And The Chocolate Factory* on real sets built at Pinewood Studios as opposed to using a lot of computer animation. Was that a big help to you?

That was one of the things that was important to me because (1) it's a movie about texture. That's what I remember from the original book, the feeling of the description and the textures. It was important for us to have them be real. And a couple of the kids hadn't done movies or anything, so (2) having real sets was really important.

This version of Roald Dahl's story fits with the other films you've made with Johnny Depp but they tend to show quite extreme situations don't they?

(3) We've got lots of problems, and we like to work them out in films!

How important was it to have the co-operation of the Dahl family and his widow Felicity on this movie?

(4) Very important. I was more nervous of showing them the movie even than the studio because it was their baby. I was really nervous, but they were great all the way through. Felicity's really a great person.

What do you say to the suggestions that Johnny's Willy Wonka bears an uncanny resemblance to Michael Jackson?

(5) Actually that's false. We based it on LaToya.

You cast one actor, Deep Roy, as all of the Oompa-Loompas. How come?

One way to do it would be to hire a cast of Oompa-Loompas, or (6) the more modern approach would probably be to do them all with computer animation. But I felt the human element was still important. Deep looks like an Oompa-Loompa to me. (7) Also it seemed to fit with the Roald Dahl universe. There's something weird about it that seemed appropriate to me.

In the last few years (8) your films seem to have become less dark. What do you put this down to – parenthood, perhaps?

Yeah, it's watching *The Teletubbies* and The Wiggles[1]. I just have a much cheerier outlook. I'm a happy person!

1   *Burton stressed that it was a movie about texture.*
2   ....
3   ....
4   ....
5   ....
6   ....
7   ....
8   ....

[1] *The Teletubbies* is a children's TV programme in the UK. *The Wiggles* are an Australian band who perform music for children.

65 Read this account of an actor's first job and fill each gap with a suitable word (pronoun, *wh*-word, *that*, or preposition). Can any gaps be left blank?

Simon Letterston, actor

My first job

I was six months out of drama school and I'd been unemployed for the whole time. Then I saw an advert in Actor's Weekly – 'Fresh talent wanted for period film' – and wondered (1) .... *whether* .... to apply. Before I made up my mind, I called the production company and indicated (2) .... that I was interested. They assured (3) .... they would take my application seriously. I also phoned a friend who'd worked with this company to find out (4) .... the pay and conditions were like, and he reassured (5) .... they really weren't bad.

So before long I'd sent in my résumé, hardly daring to imagine (6) .... it would catch somebody's eye, and to my delight I was called for audition 48 hours later. I chose a passage from a French play, and learnt it by heart. I was terrified on the day of the audition, but I reminded (7) .... I had nothing to lose, and just needed to show them (8) .... I could do. I don't remember (9) .... happened when my turn came, but it must have been OK.

They notified (10) .... within a week (11) .... I had been successful, and I've never looked back.

66 Complete the punctuation in this extract from a novel.

> Ella came back into the room.
> Have you seen him? Alex asked, and she nodded.
> He was in the garden she replied so I went up and told him.
> What exactly did you say asked Alex.
> I said I wasn't going to Sweden with him – I thought it was better to be direct replied Ella.
> Alex looked impatient and asked But how did he react
> Not very well of course said Ella and she smiled knowingly.

67 Report these short conversations using the verbs in italics.

1 *check   deny*

SUE: You were here this morning, weren't you, Philip?

PHILIP: Yes, why?

SUE: Well, it's just that there are coffee stains on the carpet upstairs and they weren't there this morning. Did you spill your coffee?

PHILIP: No, I haven't been upstairs!

Sue checked whether Philip had been at home and told him about new coffee stains on the carpet upstairs. Philip...

2 *inform   assume   reassure*

MANAGER: I have to tell you that the company has been forced to close this factory with immediate effect.

EMPLOYEE: So we'll all be losing our jobs then?

MANAGER: I guarantee that we will relocate all workers to our other larger factories if that is what they wish.

3 *confide   agree   warn*

SARAH: Don't tell anyone, but I think he's made the wrong decision.

JO: I can't help agreeing with you.

SARAH: But I wouldn't say anything if I were you, he'd be furious!

4 *require   expect*

MANAGER: You are to be at work by 7.00.

EMPLOYEE: So we'll be able to leave at 3.00?

MANAGER: It is our expectation that you will stay till 3.30.

5 *point out   confess   suggest*

MAN: Sorry to trouble you, Mrs Farmer, but your car is blocking mine.

NEIGHBOUR: I'm afraid I've locked the key inside.

MAN: You'd better call the breakdown service then.

6 *complain   understand   consider*

DEFENDANT: It's not right! I haven't been treated fairly!

FRIEND: I must say I thought that the evidence was incomplete.

DEFENDANT: Exactly!

FRIEND: Unfortunately, Jack, it isn't up to us. As far as the judge is concerned, the case is closed.

68 In this email, Tim is telling his boss about his decision to leave the company. Choose the correct items to fill the gaps. Sometimes more than one of the alternatives is possible.

Dear Matt

I hope things have been going well during my summer break.

I'm afraid I've got some news which you may not be very pleased about. I've reached (1) .... my recent health problems have been largely due to the stress of my current role with the company – I'm finding the travel and the workload too much. So I've (2) .... leave as soon as possible.

This has been a difficult decision for me and I haven't forgotten that you (3) .... it might be a tough period, but I've found it harder to cope than I thought.

As the current project is due to finish in one month's time, there is (4) .... I might be able to leave before the end of the three-month notice period in my contract. I'd be grateful if you could let me know your views on that.

With very best wishes,

Tim

Dear Tim

Your news, I must admit, came as a shock to me. It's only a few months since you (5) .... extra work, and you seemed keen then. I don't suppose I can (6) .... it might be worth staying and we'll see if we can make your life easier? If not, I'm afraid (7) .... you will be able to leave earlier than your notice period, but (8) .... I'll do my best.

Assuming that you are really serious about this, I can only (9) .... you have been an excellent member of the team and I will be sorry to lose you. Please can we meet at 10.00 on your first day back to discuss this – thanks.

Matt

1 a the conclusion that   b the conclusion   c the conclusion to
2 a made the decision that   b made the decision to   c made the decision
3 a warned to me that   b warned me that   c warned that
4 a the issue of whether   b the issue of   c the issue as to whether
5 a volunteered to take on   b volunteered taking on   c volunteered that you would take on
6 a persuade that   b persuade you that   c persuade to you that
7 a there's no guarantee that b there's no guarantee which c there's no guarantee as to
8 a let me reassure   b let me reassure you   c let me reassure you that
9 a tell you that   b say that   c say to you that

69 A few days later, Matt is telling a colleague about the meeting with Tim. Fill each gap with an appropriate adjective from the box followed by *that*, a *wh*-word, or a preposition.

| abusive   adamant   certain   complimentary   critical   dismissive   sure   sympathetic |

TINA: So what happened? How did it go?

MATT: Well, I told him I wasn't (1) .... *sure whether* .... he really wanted to leave.

TINA: And what did he say?

MATT: Well, he was (2) .... it was the right thing for him to do and the discussion was quite amicable. I was (3) .... him when he wanted to talk about his health issues, and at first he was (4) .... the experience of working for the company.

TINA: But then?

MATT: It got awkward, I'm afraid. He was (5) .... my suggestions about reducing his workload, and then he insisted I could have made things better for him earlier on.

TINA: Oh dear. What happened next?

MATT: He started to get very (6) .... the way the company works, and I wasn't (7) .... to say to him. And then, when he started becoming (8) .... other members of the team, I called a halt to the meeting.

TINA: Good thing too!

70 Report the direct speech using the verbs in italics.

1   *urge   swear   insist*
'Please join us at the restaurant tonight, Jill. Everyone, believe me, everyone will be there and they all want to see you. Listen, you must come – I'll take you there myself!'

Mike urged Jill to come out with everyone that night. He ....

....

2   *announce   volunteer   invite*
'It's Marta's birthday. I'm going to call in and surprise her at home. I'll go and get some flowers and chocolate – will you join me outside her house in 20 minutes?'

It was Marta's birthday, and Pete ....

....

3   *long   hope   reveal*
I would love to live in a warmer climate – I don't want to wear jumpers and coats all the time. Maybe I'll get the chance soon – my company is thinking of opening a branch in Greece.'

Teresa ....

....

4   *suggest   offer   recommend*
'You should read something by JK Rowling I'll lend you her first novel if you like. It's worth reading the whole series if you enjoy that one.'

Bob ....

....

71A Read this extract from a newspaper article about an embarrassing moment for a politician. Can you reconstruct the politician's original note?

Look who's napping!

Our new MP was spotted taking a quick nap in the middle of a long meeting at a recent summit.
Our crafty journalist also spotted a note the MP had written to his secretary. The note said he would fall asleep if the meeting went on much longer. It's tough at the top, isn't it?

I ....
....
....

71B Here are other comments and asides that might be made in long, difficult meetings. Using the prompts given, report the direct speech or write sentences with a similar meaning.

1

Can we bring this session to an end? I'm starving!

2

We mustn't let them know what we're planning!

3

I can't hear what he's saying, can you?

4

It seems unlikely that we'll be able to agree.

5

Why do they keep disagreeing?

1 He wondered ....
2 She wrote ....
3 She admitted ....
4 She doubted ....
5 He was uncertain ....

72 Look at this humorous version of a pre-nuptial agreement[1]. Complete the agreement with appropriate adjectives or verbs from the box. You may need to use some words more than once. You can add *should* before some of the verbs.

adjectives: advisable   conceivable   essential   imperative   important
verbs: agree   be   not blame   choose   promise   refer   undertake   use

---

Pre-relationship agreement

The first partner, referred to as 'She', being of sound mind agrees to the following with the second partner, referred to as 'He':

No secrecy

(i)   At the beginning of the relationship, on their first date, it is important that each partner (1) ...should promise... (vb) to tell the other about any current girl or boyfriends, phobias and fears, or strange political beliefs.

(ii) Furthermore, it is (2) .... (adj) that each partner promise to reveal any fanatical obsessions with pets, careers, and/or organised sports.

(iii) It is absolutely crucial that each partner (3) .... (vb) aware that failure to reveal the above information will result in the immediate termination of the relationship.

No blame

(i)   It is (4) .... (adj) that the couple guarantee not to hold the person who arranged their first date responsible if the occasion is not a complete success.

(ii) It is even more crucial that one partner (5) .... (vb) the other for any incompatibility which becomes apparent during the early stages of the relationship.

Defining the relationship

(i)   If the relationship proceeds past the first date, it is (6) .... (adj) that each partner use the following terminology in describing their dating:
  • For the first 30 days, it is suggested that the term 'going out' (7) .... (vb).
  • After the first 60 days, it is advisable that each partner (8) .... (vb) the terms 'girl' or 'boyfriend' and that their acquaintances (9) .... (vb) to them as 'a couple'.

(ii) If both parties consent, it is (10) .... (adj) that this timetable be accelerated, provided that if either partner 'gets too serious', the other partner may end the relationship on the grounds of 'moving too fast'.

---

[1] *A pre-nuptial agreement* is a legally-binding contract between a couple who are about to get married. The agreement outlines the financial arrangements should the couple separate or divorce at some time in the future.

73A Read these guidelines on workplace relationships for managers. Which of the guidelines (1–7) do you think are most sensible?

Guidelines on workplace relationships

Recently, large organisations have been trying to discourage romantic relationships between their employees, because when such relationships go wrong, claims of harassment and wrongful dismissal can lead to costly legal cases. In response to this concern, a committee was asked to come up with recommendations and advice for managers. Below are some of the committee's informal guidelines for the management of large public companies:

1 Do not attempt to ban workplace relationships completely.

2 Accept the fact that such relationships will happen.

3 Discourage relationships between managers and their subordinates.

4 Make it clear that if a relationship develops between employees in the same department, one of the employees will be moved to a different department.

5 If a relationship adversely affects employees' work, the employees concerned should be warned and possibly dismissed.

6 If relationship problems arise, try to solve them amicably before resorting to disciplinary measures.

7 Explain guidelines clearly to all staff and introduce them gradually.

73B Rewrite three of the guidelines that you agree with using some of these verbs: *advise, feel, propose, recommend, urge.*

Example:

We advise that management should not try to ban workplace relationships completely.

1 ....

2 ....

3 ....

73C Now give your opinions on three other guidelines using some of the adjectives in the box.

> amazed appalling concerned crucial disappointed
> important inconceivable surprised vital

Examples:

It's inconceivable that a manager (should) discourage workplace relationships.

I am concerned that a manager imagines / should imagine he can discourage relationships.

1 ....

2 ....

3 ....

74 Complete these short dialogues with ideas of your own. Include *should* in your answer, but put it in brackets if it can be left out.

"

a A: Have you seen Mario lately?

   B: Yes, I saw him yesterday.

   A: I thought he looked terrible.

   B: Me, too. In fact, I suggested (1) ....

b A: The company is in serious financial difficulties. We urge that the board give our suggestions their careful consideration.

   B: What do you propose, exactly?

   A: I propose that, in future, every employee (2) ....

   Furthermore, I advise that no new employees (3) .... in the current year.

c A: The point is that this computer has never worked since I bought it.

   B: In situations like this, sir, we request that the customer should phone the helpline.

   A: I've phoned the helpline – they were most unhelpful. I insist that (4) ....

d A: Did you hear about Mike's flat being burgled?

   B: Terrible, isn't it? He didn't know what to do.

   A: I recommended (5) ....

e JUDGE: Before passing sentence, do you have anything to say?

   CRIMINAL: Only that I apologise for all the damage I have done.

   JUDGE: In that case and in view of the severity of the offence, I direct that you
             (6) .... a minimum of seven years.

f A: Hello, Mrs Morant? This is the attendance officer from Joe's school.

   B: Oh no, he's not in trouble again, is he?

   A: I'm afraid I have to tell you he's been late every day this week.

   B: I'm very sorry.

   A: I should remind you that the school rules stipulate that (7) ....

   B: We'll make sure it doesn't happen again.

"

75 Complete these extracts from newspaper headlines using the correct form – singular or plural – of appropriate verbs from the box. Sometimes both forms are possible.

be   build   have   open   ~~promise~~   wear   win

1
Council environment team *promises / promise* **24-hour graffiti clean-up.**

2
Only a fraction of the workforce .... the right qualification.

3
1 in 3 women .... **the wrong shoes.**

4
Real Madrid .... **their fifth match in a row.**

5
One of Britain's top public schools .... *its doors to girls.*

6
New York Times .... most famous US newspaper.

7
Fiat .... **on Punto's success with new model.**

76 Look at the verb agreement in the underlined sentences of these short conversations. Correct any errors by writing ✗ and the correction at the side. If the line is correct, write ✓ and add any alternative verb form.

a A: (1) Where is my glasses? (2) Have anybody seen my glasses?
   B: No, sorry.
   A: (3) So neither of you have seen them?
   C: Afraid not.

b A: (4) Every song on your CD sounds the same to me.
   B: That's because you're old, Mum.
   A: Yeah, Mum. (5) To us, each of the songs are completely unique.

c A: (6) A lot of people I know says the university is excellent.
   B: It is. (7) The staff in the economics department is very well-qualified.
   A: Is that what you're studying?
   B: (8) Yes, economics are my best subject.

d A: (9) The news were very interesting this morning.
      (10) Apparently diabetes is getting more and more common.
   B: (11) That's because the medical profession is finding it easier to diagnose the illness now.

e A: (12) The number of burglaries in our area have doubled in the last three years.
   B: It's terrible. (13) The couple who live next door to me were burgled just last week.

f   A: (14) <u>Press intrusion into people's lives is getting beyond a joke</u>.

   B: You're right. (15) <u>In fact the media in general are guilty of invading people's privacy</u>.

g   A: (16) <u>There's lots of people who use their mobile phones while they're driving</u>.

   B: (17) <u>I know, and as far as I can see the police isn't doing much to stop it</u>.

1   *X / are*   10   ....

2   11   ....

3   12   ....

4   13   ....

5   14   ....

6   15   ....

7   16   ....

8   17   ....

9   ....

77   Use your own ideas to complete the sentences.

1   A lot of people I know ....

2   The outskirts of the town where I live ....

3   I think statistics ....

4   Banning smoking in public places ....

5   I'm one of those people who ....

6   What worries me most about the future ....

78   Look at these advertisements. Why is each of the underlined verbs singular or plural?

1   Discover why Snow Drops <u>is</u> whiter than white.

2   DELTA <u>FLY</u> TO AMERICA FROM MORE EUROPEAN CITIES THAN ANYONE ELSE.

A M S T E R D A M	N E W Y O R K	D L 1 4
L O N D O N	A T L A N T A	D L 6 3
P A R I S	M I A M I	D L 9 2
M A D R I D	D A L L A S	D L 2 9

3

Essex Libraries <u>has</u> been lending CDs and DVDs for quite a while.

4

Windows <u>is</u> shutting down…

5   **See how the other half <u>live</u>.**

79 Read this text about The Gotan Project, a music group which plays electronic tango music. Match each sentence beginning (1–8) with an appropriate ending (a–h), and complete with the correct form of one of the verbs from the box. One verb should be made passive.

Example:
One of the most interesting things about The Gotan Project is the way they combine traditional and modern music.

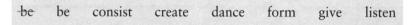

~~be~~	be	consist	create	dance	form	give	listen

1 ~~One of the most interesting things about The Gotan Project...~~
2 The band...
3 XL Recordings, their record company, ...
4 This unique trio, based in Paris, ...
5 The music press worldwide...
6 A typical Gotan audience...
7 The majority of people at their concerts just...
8 A few young people get up and move about, but usually it's the older generation who...

a ...a well-respected dance music label.
b ...their unusual sound by combining dub and hip-hop influences with the sounds of talented Argentinian tango musicians
c ...in the late nineties by Philippe Cohen-Solal.
d ...of people of all ages.
e ...the tango in the aisles or at the front of the concert hall.
f ~~...the way they combine traditional and modern music.~~
g ...their live performances ecstatic reviews
h ...to the music, clapping along or swaying in their seats.

80 Read this short text and answer the questions.

There can be little doubt that what is required to deal with the increasing threat of international terrorism are new laws and new powers for the police. Many politicians are demanding an extension to the period of time during which suspects can be detained without trial.
A government sub-committee is currently working on updating existing legislation in this area. Each of the committee members has significant experience of such work.

1 Where might you read a text like this?
2 What tells you that this short text is written in formal language?
3 How could you change the text to make it sound more informal?

Nouns
(compound nouns and noun phrases)

81 Complete these short conversations using compound nouns or noun phrases made from the words in brackets.

a A: I hear you've got a new job. Congratulations!

B: Thanks, but it's nothing special – it's just an ordinary (1) ....nine-to-five job.... (job which starts at nine and goes on until five).

A: It's in a (2) .... (shop which sells books), isn't it?

B: Yes, Red Lion Books in the (3) .... (part of town that is in the centre).

b A: So, tell me again. What do I need to make Chicken Tonnato?

B: OK, you'll need some (4) .... (breasts which are from a chicken) and a (5) .... (tin which contains tuna). You'll also need to get some (6) .... (purée which is made from tomatoes).

A: OK, how much?

B: Two (7) .... (cups which are full).

c A: I'm making a (8) .... (list of things to buy at the shops). Is there anything you want me to get?

B: We need some tea and some coffee.

A: Do you want (9) .... (bags which contain tea) or (10) .... (leaves from a tea plant)?

d A: Have you seen my (11) .... (case I keep my glasses in)?

B: I think I saw it lying on the (12) .... (table in the kitchen).

A: I've looked there and I didn't see it.

B: Have you looked in the (13) .... (bedroom which the children sleep in)?

82 Choose the more natural compound nouns and noun phrases in these texts.

A

(1) Warm-up exercises / Exercises for warm-up lower (2) blood pressure / pressure of blood, improve (3) the flow of blood / the blood flow to the heart, and increase (4) muscle temperature / the temperature of muscles. You should do (5) a five-minute warm-up / a warm-up of five minutes at an easy (6) walking pace / pace of walking before stretching. Never stretch cold muscles or you risk tearing them.

B

Sure, you've heard of the Internet, but what is it exactly? Simply put, the Internet is a (7) computer network / collection of computers that are all connected to each other. Some people, typically at universities and large companies, have (8) 24-hour connections / connections open for 24 hours a day, while others use a modem to link their (9) home computers / computers they have at home for a certain amount of time each day.

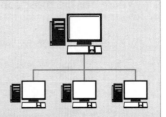

C **MINISTER ACCUSED OF** (10) <u>**FINANCIAL FRAUD COVER-UP /**
COVER-UP OF FINANCIAL FRAUD</u>

D **Supermarket launches** (11) <u>**free school computer handout scheme /**
scheme to hand out free computers to schools</u>

83 Look at the underlined phrases in these short dialogues. Correct any errors. If the phrase is correct, write ✓.

"

a A: I love that lamp. Where did you get it?
   B: I made it out of an old (1) <u>bicycle's wheel</u>.

b A: James starts at the Central High in September.
   B: Is that a (2) <u>boy school</u>?
   A: No, it's mixed.

c A: So, you didn't win the race?
   B: No, but we were the (3) <u>runners-up</u>. Believe it or not, (4) <u>my parents-in-laws</u> won it!

d A: I want to try and get fit, so I'm going to buy an (5) <u>exercises machine</u>.
   B: You don't need a machine, you can just do (6) <u>sits-up and push-ups</u> on your (7) <u>kitchen's floor</u>.

"

1 ....   5 ....
2 ....   6 ....
3 ....   7 ....
4 ....

84 Think about your home. List all the compound nouns you can think of in answer to the following questions.

1 Where are the books kept?
   Most of the books are on bookshelves, but there are a few in a small bookcase in my room.

2 What are your two favourite rooms?
   ....

3 What electrical appliances are there in your kitchen?
   ....

4 Where are the most comfortable places to sit?
   ....

5 What can you see from your front door?
   ....

Articles
(a/an, the, zero article, one)

85 Fill the gaps in these short conversations using the nouns and noun phrases in the boxes. Use the articles before each gap as a guide.

a

| friend of mine   Managing Director   Sales Executive |

A: Genevieve, this is Rexa. She's a (1) ....
B: Nice to meet you, Rexa. What do you do?
A: I'm the (2) .... of a small advertising agency. What about you?
B: I'm a (3) .... for a clothing company.

b

| holiday I'll never forget   horizon   summer of 2001   summer we spent in Denmark |

A: Do you remember the (4) .... ?
B: Of course! It's a (5) .... It was the (6) .... , wasn't it?
A: That's right. Blue sky to the (7) .... , all day, every day!

c

| Japanese cars   new car   of those   past   Toyota |

A: I've just bought a (8) ....
B: Oh, have you? What is it?
A: It's a (9) ....
B: Nice. Didn't you have one (10) .... in the (11) .... ?
A: Yes, I did. I've always liked (12) ....

d

| hostas   mixture   sun   sun and shade   Sunday morning |

A: Nice to see the (13) .... ! Gardening again?
B: Yes, I love spending a (14) .... in the garden.
A: What are you planting?
B: They're called (15) .... – they have big leaves and lovely flowers.
A: Why are you putting them there?
B: They like a (16) .... of (17) ....

e

| first Monday after my birthday   future   morning |

A: Haven't seen you for ages! When did you start your new job?
B: It was the (18) ....
A: And how's it going?
B: Really well, but the journey is awful in the (19) ....
A: Do you drive?
B: Yes, but it takes ages. In (20) .... I think I'll take the train.

86 Fill the gaps in this article about mobile phone usage among young people. Use *a/an*, *the* or Ø (the zero article). Sometimes more than one answer is possible.

(1) ....Ø........ new technologies change how we conduct our lives. (2) .... mobile phone is central to the lives of (3) .... young people. 97% of females and 92% of males have access to (4) .... mobile phone. (5) .... mobile phones are a vital tool for young people's social lives – the phone is (6) .... part of their person and identity, not just (7) .... piece of equipment. More than four fifths of females and seven out of ten males 'could not bear to be without' their mobile phones. How do they use them, and how does this compare with (8) .... other forms of communication?

Three quarters use their mobiles to speak to (9) .... friends at least daily, and one in six do so more than five times (10) .... day. However, texting is (11) .... most frequent form of communication: nine out of ten text at least daily, and over half (54%) do so more than five times in every 24-hour period. Texting was the 'surprise' development out of (12) .... new technology, and it is (13) .... central part of young people's social interaction.

Nearly nine out of ten have access to (14) .... Internet on (15) .... personal computer; more than four out of five females and just under seven out of ten males have access to (16) .... email.

(17) .... younger teenagers use both their computers and their mobile phones to surf (18) .... net and to send email, but post-16s primarily use their personal computers rather than their mobiles for both internet use and email.

(19) .... mobile phones provide (20) .... sense of security: 87% of females and 68% of males agree that 'having my mobile phone makes me feel safer and more secure'.

87 Fill the gaps in these short dialogues with *a/an*, *the*, Ø (the zero article), or *one*.

a A: You'll never guess who I saw in Covent Garden.

   B: Who?

   A: Kate Winslet.

   B: Not (1) .... Kate Winslet? When?

   A: (2) .... evening last week. I was out for (3) .... evening with (4) .... Smiths, old family friends, and there she was!

   B: Wow! She's (5) .... wonderful actor, but she'll never be (6) .... Marilyn Monroe.

b TEENAGER: What's that?

   FATHER: (7) .... LP. We used to listen to (8) .... music on these before (9) .... CD was invented.

   TEENAGER: Well I just use (10) .... MP3 player. This one only cost (11) .... Euro – as long as you bought (12) .... DVD player at the same time!

c A: This looks wonderful! What is it?

   B: It's (13) .... Italian dish, made with pasta and olives. Just 15 minutes from (14) .... start to (15) .... finish! Do you want (16) .... piece of bread with that, or two?

   A: I'll start with (17) .... , but I'll probably come back for (18) .... other!

d A: There's (19) .... Graham Potter on (20) .... phone for you. He's phoning because he heard about your interest in archery and wants to know if you'd like to become (21) .... FITA member.

   B: (22) .... what member?

   A: Apparently FITA is (23) .... international archery organisation.

   B: I'm still in (24) .... bath. Can you tell him to call me back?

88A Complete this joke using *this* or *the*.

One day, (1) .... boy is standing next to the sea eating an ice cream.

(2) .... other boy comes up and says, 'Do you believe in sea monsters?'

(3) .... first boy says, 'Yes, I do.'

'Well,' says (4) .... second boy, 'guess what sea monsters eat.'

'I don't know,' he says.

The second boy says, 'Fish and ships.'

88B Write a joke that you know using *this* to introduce each new person or thing.

Determiners and quantifiers

(*some, any, no, none, not any, much, many, a lot of, all, whole, very, each, every, few, little, less, fewer ...*)

89 These various formal extracts all include informal language that is not appropriate. Rewrite the underlined sections in a more formal style, with the aid of the prompts given, making any changes needed.

A   A literary extract:

The ship lay quietly in harbour, the mist curling around its proud outline. (1) <u>Nobody could hear a sound</u> from the decks, and (2) <u>there wasn't an answer</u> when people called from the harbourside. (3) <u>However much people called or searched, the fate of the passengers of the *Agnes Rose* was never revealed</u>.

1   Not *a sound could be heard*

2   no .... came

3   No amount .... ever ....

B   From a political speech:

Over the coming months, (4) <u>there'll be a lot of debate focusing</u> on the choice of my successor. (5) <u>A lot of commentators</u> will undoubtedly focus on the need for a younger leader for this great party. But, as (6) <u>lots of leaders who are departing know</u>, youth is no substitute for experience.

4   .... debate ....

5   .... commentators

6   many ....

C   From a nature documentary:

(7) <u>People don't know much</u> about the giant squid, which lives in the deepest and darkest parts of the ocean and rarely comes close to the surface. (8) <u>Humans have hardly ever seen them</u>, and when a giant squid does come near to the surface, (9) <u>fishermen don't take much notice</u>, believing only that a shark or dolphin is swimming beneath them.

7   .... is known

8   Few ....

9   .... little ....

90 Cross out any forms which are not possible in this dialogue. Sometimes all the choices are possible.

ANN: It's my sister's birthday soon and she's asked me for (1) <u>some book or other / a book / a book or other</u> about modern American art.

KATE: Really? That's not my scene at all – (2) <u>modern paintings all look the same / all modern paintings look the same / all of the modern paintings look the same</u> to me. Have you found the one she wants?

ANN: Well, (3) <u>I've had few time / I haven't had much time / I've had little time</u> this week, and I've had (4) <u>any luck / no luck</u> so far. First I tried my local bookshop, and they kept me waiting for half an hour while they searched for the book, and then told me (5) <u>there were none / not any were / there weren't any</u> left.

KATE: Oh dear. Where else have you tried?

ANN: The bookshop suggested a specialist modern art store, so I called them but there (6) <u>was no answer / weren't any answers / wasn't any answer</u>, and I haven't been able to access the Internet (7) <u>the whole week / all week / all the week</u> – it's so frustrating!

KATE: Look, let me help. There's a huge bookshop (8) <u>fewer than / less than</u> a kilometre from my office, and they have (9) <u>a large number of / many / lots of</u> books about art. Why don't you let me try for you?

ANN: Oh no, I don't want to put you to any trouble.

KATE: No, really, it's a great excuse to visit my favourite shop and (10) <u>not any / no</u> trouble at all.

91 Complete this phone conversation using a word from the box to fill each gap. You can use a word more than once.

all   entire   every   far   many   no   none   nothing

KATE: Ann, it's Kate – I'm phoning about the book.

ANN: Oh hi, Kate. Thanks ever so much. How did you get on?

KATE: Well, I tried that bookshop near my office, and the first person I spoke to was (1) .... help at all. She knew (2) .... at all about art! But as the (3) .... place was full of art books I decided to ask someone else – I really didn't believe that (4) .... of the staff could help.

ANN: What happened?

KATE: Eventually a really nice guy came up and offered to have a look for me. He said that (5) .... so often they find a title in the store that isn't on their computer system – and you were in luck!

ANN: Oh wonderful – thank you so much, Kate.

KATE: It was pretty lucky really – he said the book's been out of print for a year and there aren't (6) .... left in the shops.

ANN: (7) .... wonder it was so difficult to find!

92 Ann is telling Kate about a trip to the sales. Match each sentence beginning (1–6) with an appropriate ending (a–f), and complete with a quantifying phrase from the box.

Example:

1 I'm just back from the sales. I got to Darcy's Department store really early this morning, before anyone else.

| as anyone ~~before anyone~~ far too much not all of them no fewer than what little time |

1 ~~I'm just back from the sales. I got to Darcy's Department store really early this morning,~~ ...
2 I wanted to make sure I had as good a chance...
3 There were lots of different things I was looking for, but...
4 I was really pleased with everything I managed to get, especially considering...
5 A friend said the sale was so popular that...
6 I spent...

a ...to get some bargains.
b ...~~else.~~
c ...and hope I won't regret it.
d ...5000 people came through the doors on that morning alone.
e ...I had.
f ...were in the sale.

93 Read this news article about an unusual shopper, and fill each gap with *any*, *every*, *many* or *not*.

Most of us wouldn't regard shoplifting as an ideal retirement activity. But Dorothy Agar, 87, spent (1) .... hours in her local department store helping herself to shoes, dresses, scarves, gloves and even underwear – yet (2) .... one of the stolen items fitted her. (3) .... few weeks Dorothy made her way to John Lewis in Newcastle's main street, and almost (4) .... time she was tempted to carry something out in the plain brown bag she always carried with her. She was always caught, of course – the alarms went off at the front door virtually (5) .... time she went through them. Among her (6) .... excuses were forgetfulness, charity (she said she gave away a great (7) .... of her possessions), and poor labelling in the shop. Reluctant to bring (8) .... charges, the store manager, David Burrell, said recently that she meant no harm and that he had '(9) .... sympathy' for her addiction – to a life of crime.

94A Read this article describing how Japanese High School students spend their Saturday. Look at the information in the article and fill the gaps using the phrases in the box.

> ~~a considerable amount of time~~   a great deal of that   a substantial amount of time
> each   just over   less than   little   not much time   some

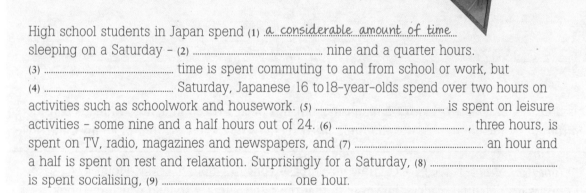

How do we spend our Saturdays?

> sleeping (9 hours, 19 minutes)
> schoolwork and housework (2 hours, 14 minutes)
> commuting (11 minutes)
> total leisure activities (9 hours, 30 minutes)
> TV, radio, magazines and newspapers
> (3 hours, 4 minutes)
> rest and relaxation (1 hour, 35 minutes)
> socialising (54 minutes)

High school students in Japan spend (1) *a considerable amount of time* sleeping on a Saturday – (2) .... nine and a quarter hours. (3) .... time is spent commuting to and from school or work, but (4) .... Saturday, Japanese 16 to 18-year-olds spend over two hours on activities such as schoolwork and housework. (5) .... is spent on leisure activities – some nine and a half hours out of 24. (6) .... , three hours, is spent on TV, radio, magazines and newspapers, and (7) .... an hour and a half is spent on rest and relaxation. Surprisingly for a Saturday, (8) .... is spent socialising, (9) .... one hour.

94B Imagine you work for a market research organisation and have collected the information in this table about people's shopping habits in a new shopping centre. Write a paragraph like the one in exercise 94A reporting your findings.

Activity	Hours: minutes
Clothes shops	1:10
Other shops	1:01
Eating and drinking	0:30
Sitting down	0:07
Talking to friends in person	0:08
Talking on mobile phone	0:15
At machine paying for parking	0:03
Average shopping trip: total	3:14

95 Correct any errors you find in these extracts from the review of a novel. Write ✓ if the extract is correct.

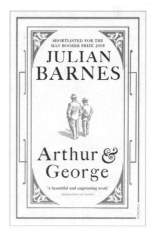

1 *Arthur and George*, that was published in 2005, is by the novelist Julian Barnes.

2 The novel is not only written by an Englishman, it is set in England, and adopts a style who's quiet formality has something distinctively English about it.

3 One of the central characters is the creator of the fictional detective Sherlock Holmes, the author, Sir Arthur Conan Doyle. The other people, none of which most readers will have heard of, are also real-life characters.

4 It would be difficult to overstate the skill with whom Barnes turns a minor event in the life of Conan Doyle into a focus for a range of cultural and personal issues.

5 The first section, which follows George and Arthur through childhood, could not have been done any better.

6 *Arthur and George* is everything good popular fiction should be: it is a readable novel written by someone whom possesses a genuine feel for language and a deep appreciation of style.

1 .... 4 ....

2 .... 5 ....

3 .... 6 ....

96 This book review was written for a magazine, but has been written in a style which is considered too formal by the editor. Rewrite the underlined sections of the review in a more informal style.

(1) <u>*Midnight Strikes* is the perfect crime novel for anyone to whom Sherlock Holmes is a hero.</u> I must warn potential readers, however, (2) <u>that the rather literary style in which the book is written will make it hard-going</u> for those used to fast-moving blockbusters. (3) <u>I suspect, in fact, that the readers to whom this book will most appeal will probably be over the age of 30.</u>

(4) <u>The story is set in the early part of the twentieth century, a time at which the general population</u> were quite unaware of the horrors of modern warfare, a state of affairs which changes dramatically as the plot develops. (5) <u>The villain of the novel devises a plan whereby he gains the trust of vulnerable people whom he meets at church.</u> Having befriended them, he gradually persuades them to part with their lifelong savings.

(6) <u>The character with whom many male readers will most closely identify is Inspector Blakeman</u>, a tough uncompromising detective whose methods are highly unconventional. Female readers may find this character hard to accept.

(7) <u>The ending, about which I can say nothing</u>, will come as a genuine surprise.

1   *Midnight Strikes is the perfect crime novel for anyone whose hero is Sherlock Holmes.*
2   ....
3   ....
4   ....
5   ....
6   ....
7   ....

97   Choose the correct items to complete these short conversations. Sometimes both answers are correct.

a   A: What kind of novels do you like reading?
     B: I've got very broad tastes. I like any novel (1) <u>that / what</u> grips me.

b   A: I'm going to buy a season ticket and watch every match.
     B: Season tickets are really expensive, you know.
     A: I don't care. I'm going to buy one (2) <u>what / whatever</u> they cost.

c   A: Here are the letters you asked for.
     B: Thank you very much.
     A: I think you'll find they contain all (3) <u>that / which</u> you need to know.

d   A: What do you like most about having a mobile phone?
     B: You can talk to anyone you like (4) <u>wherever / where</u> you are and (5) <u>when / whenever</u> you want.

e   A: I want to buy a new bike, but there are so many good offers at the moment, I just don't know which one to get.
     B: If I were you, I'd try several and buy (6) <u>which / whichever</u> feels the most comfortable.

98A Complete this online encyclopaedia entry about the history of the guitar by adding one of these relative pronouns: *who, which, when, where, that*.

ARTS | BIOGRAPHY | CULTURE | GEOGRAPHY | HISTORY | MATHEMATICS | PHILOSOPHY | SCIENCE | SOCIETY | TECHNOLOGY

A BRIEF HISTORY OF THE GUITAR

Guitar-like instruments have existed since ancient times but the first written mention is from the 14th century. The earliest form of the instrument, (1) .... had three pairs of strings plus one single string, probably originated in Spain, (2) .... , by the 16th century, it was popular among the lower classes. They could not afford the *vihuela*, an instrument (3) .... was popular with the upper classes.

The guitar in its modern form had developed by the mid-18th century, (4) .... the fifth and sixth strings were added. By this time, too, all the strings had become single rather than pairs. The guitar makers (5) .... worked in the 19th century broadened the body and changed the internal structure. The old tuning pegs, (6) .... were wooden, were replaced by modern machine heads.

The guitar was once regarded as a simple instrument (7) .... could not play classical music, but in the early 19th century, Fernando Sor started a quest (8) .... still continues today, to raise the guitar to the highest musical level.

Sor, (9) .... was one of the most prolific composers for the guitar as a 'concert' instrument, paved the way for the great Spanish player Andrés Segovia, (10) .... was to bring the guitar the popularity and respect (11) .... it now enjoys.

Today guitars come in all shapes and sizes. There is the twelve-string guitar (12) .... has six pairs of strings in standard tuning. The Hawaiian, or 'steel' guitar is laid across the knees of the player, (13) .... stops the metal strings by sliding a metal bar along the neck. The electric guitar, (14) .... was developed for popular music in the United States in the 1930s, usually has a solid body, (15) .... means that the sound of its strings has to be amplified electronically.

98B Which one of the relative pronouns you have added to the article could be omitted?

99 Read about the American guitarist Ry Cooder and add the extra information at appropriate places in the article. The extra information is given in order. Add commas wherever they are needed.

> **Ry Cooder** is a musician especially well known for his slide guitar work. He first attracted public attention in the 1960s. In recent years, Cooder has composed many film soundtracks. Cooder has also played an important role in the increased appreciation of traditional Cuban music, especially in connection with the Buena Vista Social Club recording. The recording was made by Cuban musicians. In 1999, a documentary film was made about the musicians.

1   Ry Cooder was born on March 15th, 1947 in Los Angeles.
2   In the 1960s, he played with Captain Beefheart and the Magic Band.
3   Cooder has worked mainly as a studio musician.
4   His best known film soundtrack is perhaps the one he wrote for *Paris, Texas*.
5   Ry Cooder was the producer of the Buena Vista Social Club recording.
6   The Buena Vista Social Club recording was a worldwide hit.
7   Some of the Buena Vista musicians had not played for many years.
8   The documentary was directed by Wim Wenders.
9   The documentary film was nominated for an Academy Award.

Example:
Ry Cooder, **who was born on March 15th, 1947 in Los Angeles**, is a musician especially well known for his slide guitar work.

100 Read this email from someone who is giving a friend directions to his house. Rewrite the underlined sections more economically by leaving words out, and making other changes as necessary. Which section is better not changed?

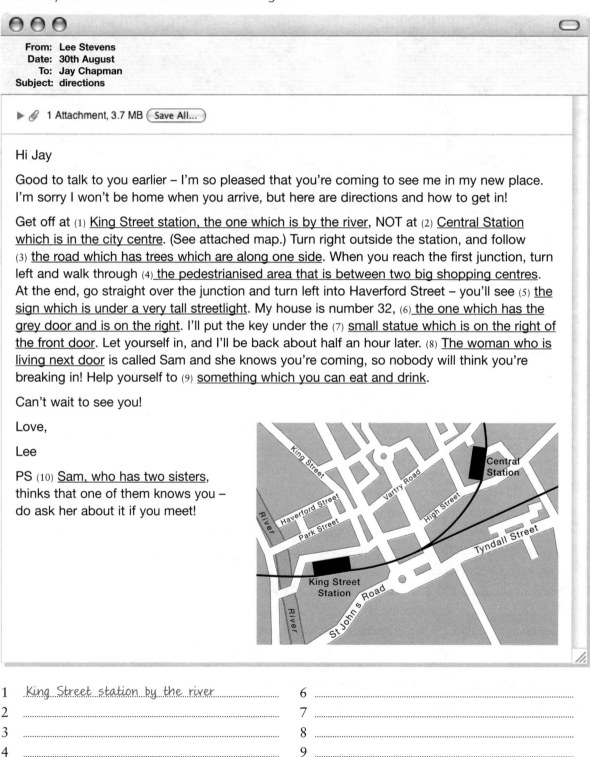

○ ○ ○

From: **Lee Stevens**
Date: **30th August**
To: **Jay Chapman**
Subject: **directions**

▶ 🖉 1 Attachment, 3.7 MB (Save All…)

Hi Jay

Good to talk to you earlier – I'm so pleased that you're coming to see me in my new place. I'm sorry I won't be home when you arrive, but here are directions and how to get in!

Get off at (1) <u>King Street station, the one which is by the river</u>, NOT at (2) <u>Central Station which is in the city centre</u>. (See attached map.) Turn right outside the station, and follow (3) <u>the road which has trees which are along one side</u>. When you reach the first junction, turn left and walk through (4) <u>the pedestrianised area that is between two big shopping centres</u>. At the end, go straight over the junction and turn left into Haverford Street – you'll see (5) <u>the sign which is under a very tall streetlight</u>. My house is number 32, (6) <u>the one which has the grey door and is on the right</u>. I'll put the key under the (7) <u>small statue which is on the right of the front door</u>. Let yourself in, and I'll be back about half hour later. (8) <u>The woman who is living next door</u> is called Sam and she knows you're coming, so nobody will think you're breaking in! Help yourself to (9) <u>something which you can eat and drink</u>.

Can't wait to see you!

Love,

Lee

PS (10) <u>Sam, who has two sisters,</u> thinks that one of them knows you – do ask her about it if you meet!

1 <u>King Street station by the river</u>   6 ....

2 ....   7 ....

3 ....   8 ....

4 ....   9 ....

5 ....   10 ....

70

101 Add the country names to these extracts from travel brochures choosing from the options in the box. Then expand the notes in italics to make complete sentences.

America ~~Australia~~ Brazil China India Luxembourg

1  After two days in the city, we take a flight north to the country's vast interior. Our first stop is the grandest sight of all. *Uluru / striking volcanic hill / hundreds of kilometres / major city / attracts thousands / visitors /* ....Australia................*'s Northern Territory.*

Uluru, a striking volcanic hill hundreds of kilometres from any major city, attracts thousands of visitors to Australia's Northern Territory.

2 .... */ only country / northern Europe / no coastline.* We spend a day exploring the architecture and museums of the capital city before heading north into Belgium.

....

3 *Death Valley / California / made / National Park in 1994 / contains* ....*'s lowest point 86m / sea level / covers over 13,000 square kilometres.* We don't spend long here, just long enough to experience the other-worldly quality of this sub-sea-level land.

....

4 *The Amazon River Basin / more than 1000 tributaries / comprising over half of* ....*'s land area / dominant geographical feature / country.* Why not try one of our daily pleasure flights and see the vast expanses of water from the air?

....

5  Looking for a never-to-be-forgotten trip? .... , *bordered / north / Himalaya mountain range / dominated / vast river systems and plateaus further south / country / extraordinary natural features / rich cultural history.* We offer a range of holidays to cater for every taste in this varied and fascinating country.

....

6 Finish your tour of this fast-changing country with a once in a lifetime visit to its capital. *Beijing / lying / plain / north-eastern* .... , */ capital city since 1421.* We take you on an unforgettable tour of the Forbidden City, and show you parts of the city where the traditional way of life goes on in the shadow of modern development.

....

102A Look at the article about nanotechnology[1]. The article is in three parts with different tasks for each section. In this first section choose the more natural alternatives. Sometimes both are equally acceptable.

Brush up on your nanotechnology

The world's smallest brushes (1) <u>have been created by researchers in the US, with bristles more than a thousand times finer than a human hair / with bristles more than a thousand times finer than a human hair, have been created by researchers in the US.</u>

The brushes can be used for sweeping, painting minute structures and even cleaning up pollutants in water.

The bristles' secret is the carbon nanotube, (2) <u>that is / which is</u>, a tiny straw-like molecule just 30 billionths of a metre across. These are incredibly tough and yet flexible enough that they will yield when pushed from the side. The scientists grow bristles from hot, carbon-laden gas on to a material finer than baby's hair, (3) <u>that is / namely</u>, carbon silicide.

102B Choose the best verb from the box to fill each gap, using a participle (-*ed* or -*ing*) form as appropriate.

be   coat   dip   include   know   ~~lead~~   pick   publish

The researchers, (1) ....*led*............. by scientist Pulickel Ajayan from Rensselaer Polytechnic Institute in Troy, New York, reported their work in the journal *Nature Materials*, (2) .... yesterday.

The team, (3) .... internationally for showing how carbon nanotubes can be grown controllably, has now used the trick to make nanobrushes shaped like toothbrushes, bottle brushes and cotton-buds. Like normal brushes, the nano varieties have many uses, (4) .... sweeping up piles of nano-dust. And brushes (5) .... into a solution of iron oxide can be used to paint tiny structures – the minute brush hairs (6) .... up the oxide particles which can then be wiped on to a bare surface.

In another of their demonstrations, the researchers show that with the bristles (7) .... in absorbent materials, the brushes will soak up poisonous atoms from contaminated water. And the carbon brushes could end up with larger-scale uses, too. Carbon nanotubes, (8) .... able to conduct electricity, could be used in electric motors.

[1] *nanotechnology* = the science of the microsopically tiny

02C Fill the gaps using *and*, *or*, or *with*.

However, the scientists, (1) .... concerns already being expressed about nanotechnology and its effect on the environment, will have to make sure their brushes do not lose bristles in the environment – and have already started testing how easily they can be pulled off.

From prehistory to nanotechnology

It seems likely that brushes, (2) .... at least their simple ancient equivalents, were among the first inventions of our ancestors. The oldest surviving example, believed to be the property of some ancient hunter (3) .... cave artist, dates from 30,000 years ago.

It seems fitting that miniature versions of these should be a feature of the growing field of nanotechnology.

---

103 A few years later, a nanotechnologist receives an award for his achievements. Use the notes on the right to complete his acceptance speech, avoiding repetition of names and nouns.

I am honoured to receive this award. I have tried, with my work in nanotechnology, (1) *the science of the impossibly small* , to make advances to protect the environment, improve our health, and save us time and effort. But I could not have done this work alone. There are so many dear colleagues I would like to thank.

In the beginning, there was Dr Jana Verwoerd, (2) .... She first showed me how carbon, (3) ....

Then (4) .... Jamie Fussell gave me contacts in the world of industry, and several of his students helped to keep my enthusiasm for nanotechnology alive and burning. And, of course, Dr Katya Bubskya, (5) ....

But my greatest thanks are reserved for (6) .... Anna, without whom none of this would have been possible.

Thank you from the bottom of my heart.

1 Nanotechnology is the science of the impossibly small.

2 Dr Jana Verwoerd is director of the Institute of Carbon Studies.
   Dr Jana Verwoerd raised my interest in the topic.

3 Carbon is a wonderful ancient substance.
   Carbon could be used in ways we had only dreamed of.

4 My close friend is Jamie Fussell.
   My mentor is Jamie Fussell.

5 Dr Katya Bubskya is one of the world's leading authorities in the field.
   Dr Katya Bubskya encouraged me to publish my work to the world.

6 My dear wife is Anna.
   My colleague is Anna.

104   Rewrite any of these sentences which are incorrect. If a sentence is correct, write ✓.

1 Seeing her twin brother for the first time for nearly thirty years, Jorge burst into tears.
   Seeing her twin brother, Jorge, for the first time in thirty years, Maria burst into tears.

2 Laughing and crying at the same time, passers-by were moved by this emotional reunion
   between Jorge and Maria.

   ....

3 Having been separated in their early teens, foster families had brought up the twins in different
   parts of the country.

   ....

4 Wishing to not upset the children, neither foster family had spoken about the other twin.

   ....

5 Once accustomed to her new family, Maria lived a normal happy life.

   ....

6 Leaving school, she went to university where she studied politics and economics.

   ....

7 Having graduated, a large company took her on as a management trainee.

   ....

8 Running away from home, Jorge was unhappy in his new family.

   ....

9 Stealing some money from a shop, the police arrested Jorge and he went to prison for a year.

   ....

10 On coming out of prison, Jorge found himself a job and got married.

   ....

11 Twenty years later, watching TV, he saw a programme about people looking for lost relatives,
    deciding to try to find his sister.

   ....

05A Read this text about Catherine Cookson, a prolific popular novelist who wrote about life in the North-East of England at the beginning of the 20th century. Replace the underlined sections with appropriate participle clauses or reduced clauses.

(1) <u>As times were very hard</u>, Catherine's mother, Kate, would be sent out begging. (2) <u>Because she was more likely to arouse sympathy</u>, it was generally Kate who was sent. (3) <u>She had been born with a deformed foot and as a result</u> had been left with a permanent limp. (4) <u>With nothing on her feet</u>, she went to better-off neighbourhoods to knock on doors and ask for bread. (5) <u>When she reached the age of 12</u>, her older sister Sarah was put into service[1]. (6) <u>Despite the fact that she was paid very little</u>, she did not starve because her board and lodgings were provided.

1 *Times being very hard, Catherine's mother, Kate, would be sent out begging.*
2 ....
3 ....
4 ....
5 ....
6 ....

05B Continue Sarah's story by expanding these prompts into full sentences. Use participle clauses or reduced clauses where possible.

1 terrified of stepfather / Sarah happy to get out of the house
   Terrified / Being terrified of her stepfather, Sarah was happy to get out of the house.
2 eldest child / she suffered most from father's violent behaviour.
   ....
3 one occasion / before come home day off / visit aunt in Newcastle.
   ....
4 missed the last bus home / stayed overnight in city.
   ....
5 arrive home / stepfather beat her / did not believe her story.
   ....

[1] *put into service* = sent to be a servant

106 Read this extract from an email written by an 18-year-old boy who is making plans for his future. Answer the questions.

1 What made the writer decide to go to Australia?
2 Why do the writer's parents expect him to go straight to university and get a well-paid job?
3 What can the writer's parents say to stop him going?
4 Why does the writer need to work in his local supermarket?
5 Do you think he is really keen to stack shelves in the supermarket? Why? / Why not?

> Seeing that documentary about Australia on TV last night, I decided that I am definitely going to go travelling next year. The problem is my Mum and Dad are dead against the idea. Having made sacrifices for me, they now expect me to go straight to university and then find myself a well-paid job, without thinking about what I really want to do.
>
> But I've made up my mind to go anyway, whatever they say. I can pay for my air fare by stacking shelves in my local supermarket. I'm sure I can earn enough money before next year without having to work more than a couple of evenings a week.

107 Now think about situations involving yourself or members of your family. Complete these sentences using ideas of your own.

1 Not wishing to upset anyone, ...

2 Having forgotten to ....

3 Since I / she / he left home ....

4 Before telling ....

5 Unaware of my plans, ...

6 Without thinking about the problems that might occur, ...

7 On arriving home that night, ...

8 What with not getting on with my brother / sister, ...

9 A little ashamed of what I had done, ...

10 With the family being so short of money, ...

08A Read this newspaper article about a show jumping accident. Add the missing items (a–h).

Accident spoils champion's chances

20-year-old PA and local favourite Laura Johnson won last year's show jumping trials and (1) .... became the youngest winner for over 25 years. She won by a clear margin and (2) .... again this year.

Many commentators claim that the only way to succeed in any type of horseriding arena is to live with horses from an early age, and (3) .... , growing up on a farm which ran pony trekking as a sideline. She has represented her area nationally and competed overseas, and (4) .... , another victory looked to be a foregone conclusion in yesterday's competition.

But it was not to be. Laura slipped out of the saddle at the first fence, and managed to hang on, but (5) .... , she was never able to recover. She fell at the fourth and broke her leg in two places.

(6) .... is unusual, and she was kept in hospital for two days and nights.

Her sister, Sarah Johnson, 23, told this newspaper, 'Laura is glad to be home now. She has had lots of messages from friends and well-wishers, but has been in pain and hasn't been able to reply to them yet. She (7) .... She always enjoyed horse riding (8) .... , so I am confident she'll be back in the saddle as soon as she can.'

a	after such a poor start	e	seemed likely to do so
b	in doing so	f	Such a bad break
c	Laura did just that	g	will do so when she can
d	more than I did	h	with such an impressive record

08B Complete the following phrases to make alternative answers (a–h) for the above article.

a	after a poor start like .... *this*	e	seemed likely to do ....
b	in so	f	A bad break like ....
c	Laura did	g	will when ....
d	more than	h	with a track record as ....

109 Write a similar text about a sporting accident based on the notes provided. Include examples of *do so* and *such + a/an +* noun where possible.

Art Chambers / 110m hurdles / last Olympic Games / youngest man / break 12-second barrier. Won easily / likely again here / not to be. Hit first hurdle / fell to ground / broke left arm. Disastrous start / never going to recover / race won by compatriot Allen Layne. Coach told waiting journalists / accident not put Art off competing at the highest levels / insists as soon as able.

110 Laura's sister Sarah is helping her to get ready to go out to a party. Look at the underlined sections in the dialogue, and choose the correct options to complete the sentences. Sometimes more than one alterntaive is possible.

SARAH: Poor you – you're (1) <u>not usually like this / not your usual self / not oneself</u> at all, are you?

LAURA: No, my leg hurts and it's so annoying.

SARAH: Oh dear. Well, let me help. What can I pass you first?

LAURA: My jacket, please.

SARAH: (2) <u>Which ones / Which one / Which?</u>

LAURA: The blue one, please.

SARAH: OK, here you are. What next?

LAURA: Earrings, please. (3) <u>The silver ones / The silver one / Silver</u> with a horseshoe. And a scarf please – I've only got two so (4) <u>either of them / either / either one</u> will do, and you'll find them in the drawer next to the bed.

SARAH: Right. Anything else?

LAURA: Just sunglasses please.

SARAH: (5) <u>Which ones / Which / Which one?</u> You've got a whole drawerful[1] here!

LAURA: (6) <u>Those / Those ones / This one</u>, thanks. Do you think Liz has invited many people?

SARAH: (7) <u>I imagine so / I imagine she has / I'm sure so</u> – it's her 30th and she knows (8) <u>lots of / loads of</u> people.

LAURA: Who's helping her? It sounds like a lot to organise.

SARAH: Kat (9) <u>promised she would / promised so / promised to.</u>

LAURA: Do you think Eva will be there? I haven't seen her for ages!

SARAH: Oh, (10) <u>I'm sure she will / I expect so / I know so.</u>

LAURA: And Pete?

SARAH: (11) <u>I doubt it / I doubt that he will / I doubt so.</u> He's usually off climbing or canoeing at the weekends. He finds it hard to (12) <u>tear himself away / tear him away / tear away</u> from his hobbies! Anyway, it's time to go.

LAURA: (13) <u>So it is / Yes, it is / So it seems.</u> Ready when you are!

---

[1] *drawerful* = an informal way of saying that a drawer has a lot of a particular object in it

111 Read these short dialogues and answer the questions.

a A: I've had this email from somebody I don't know asking me for money. The person who wrote it claims that the money doesn't go to <u>themselves</u>, but to charity.

   B: Don't believe it and don't send any money. It's just a scam, and they deserve <u>to get put in prison</u>.

   1 Is the person who wrote the email male or female?
      The use of 'themselves' means we don't know.

   2 What would be the difference in meaning if B said 'to get themselves put in prison'?

   ....

b A: OK, I need someone or a couple of you to go down to London and find out what's happening. Any volunteers?

   B: <u>Kaz and myself</u> could go, couldn't we Kaz?

   3 What would be the difference in emphasis if speaker B said 'Kaz and I' instead?

   ....

c A: I wish I'd had children. I would have liked <u>some little ones</u> in my life.

   B: But you've been surrounded by <u>loved ones</u> all your life – don't forget that.

   4 What do *little ones* and *loved ones* refer to?

   ....

d A: Why did you send troops to the war zone, knowing the likely dangers?

   B: <u>One often asks oneself</u> that question, but I feel confident that the decision will prove to have been justified.

   5 Is this a formal or informal context, and how could you replace *one* and *oneself*?

   ....

e A: Have you got that book?

   B: It's really strange. I'm sure <u>I put it right in front of me</u> when we were watching TV.

   6 Can you use *myself* instead of *me* here? Why / Why not?

   ....

f A: Oscar loves that new computer game, doesn't he?

   B: Yes – <u>he just can't drag himself away</u> from it!

   7 Is *he just can't drag away* also possible? Why / Why not?

   ....

g A: So can we help ourselves to food and drink?

   B: My Dad <u>didn't say so</u>.

   8 How does the meaning change if you replace *didn't say so* with *said not to*?

   ....

112 Complete this job interview with short answers.

INTERVIEWER: So, Mr Butcher, you're interested in joining our marketing department?
APPLICANT: Yes, (1) ....
INTERVIEWER: And do you have any experience in marketing?
APPLICANT: No, I'm afraid (2) ....
INTERVIEWER: But you'd be prepared to do a training course?
APPLICANT: Yes, (3) ....
INTERVIEWER: It'd take a lot of time and commitment. Do you think you could handle that?
APPLICANT: Yes, (4) ....
INTERVIEWER: The rest of your time, you'd be working in the marketing department. I think you met the department manager, this morning.
APPLICANT: That's right, (5) .... He said you'd fill me in on the details.
INTERVIEWER: That's right, (6) .... as soon as this interview is over. Have you got any particular questions now?
APPLICANT: Yes, (7) .... Is there an online catalogue?
INTERVIEWER: Yes, (8) .... 15% of our sales come from online customers.
APPLICANT: But I expect you'd like to increase that?
INTERVIEWER: We certainly (9) ....
APPLICANT: So would you say that you value your online customers highly?
INTERVIEWER: Yes, (10) ....
APPLICANT: Then perhaps you could tell me why I haven't yet received the clothes I ordered from you seven weeks ago, and why you haven't replied to any of my emails.
INTERVIEWER: Ah, you're that Mr Butcher, are you?
APPLICANT: Yes, (11) ....

113 Read these short conversations and look at the underlined responses. Correct any incorrect responses or write ✓ if the response is correct.

"

a A: You must be very excited about starting your new job.
   B: (1) <u>Yes, I must be.</u>

b A: Are we having a managers' meeting later this week?
   B: (2) <u>We might be having.</u>
   A: So you'll be letting us know nearer the time?
   B: (3) <u>Yes, I'll be.</u>

c A: Are you still thinking of going to work in Canada?
   B: (4) <u>Yes, but my boyfriend doesn't want me to.</u>
   A: Why don't you just go for a short holiday to see if you both like it there?
   B: (5) <u>I would, but I can't afford.</u>

d   A: How did the interview go?

B: (6) <u>I didn't think they would offer me the job, but they would.</u>

A: That's fantastic, isn't it?

B: (7) <u>Yes, it is.</u>

e   A: Do you think I have a chance of getting that job?

B: (8) <u>Yes, I think.</u>

f   A: Thanks for the dictionary you bought me. It's been really useful.

B: (9) <u>I thought it would.</u>

1   Yes, I am.

2   ....

3   ....

4   ....

5   ....

6   ....

7   ....

8   ....

9   ....

114   Complete these extracts from emails with an appropriate adjective, noun or verb from the box. You may need to add *to*.

| delighted   determined   idea   mean   opportunity   plans   use   want   willing   would like |

a

I've always been interested in doing voluntary work, but I've never had the (1) ....
before. Some of my friends think I won't go through with it, but I'm quite (2) ....

b

My boss has suggested that I go on a management course next month. I'm quite (3) .... ,
as long they don't expect me to continue doing my normal work at the same time. One of my
colleagues thinks I should ask for a pay increase when I finish the course. I agree it might be a
good (4) .... , especially as I'll be taking on a management role.

c

Thanks for inviting me to visit your new factory. I'd be absolutely (5) .... , but
unfortunately I'm out of the country until October 17th. You also asked whether I have
thought about working for a different company. I have to say that at the moment I don't have
any (6) .... , but who knows how I'll be feeling this time next year?

d

Things are not going very well at work, so I've decided to look for another job. I don't really (7) .... but
I don't feel I have any choice. I'm being given more and more responsibility – and I don't even get as long a lunch
break as I (8) .... Unfortunately, I can't just leave whenever I (9) .... – I've got to give two
months' notice. My colleagues keep asking me if I've found anything yet. It's very irritating. I even lost my temper
yesterday. I didn't (10) .... , but people kept asking me the same question over and over again: 'Have
you got a new job yet?'

Adjectives

(gradable and non-gradable adjectives; participle and compound adjectives; adjective +*ing* form, *to*-infinitive, *that*-clause or *wh*-clause)

115 Read this article about controversy surrounding the opening of a new hotel. Correct any errors in the underlined sections. If the section is correct, write ✓.

> **W**hen the first guests checked in to the new 64-storey Shallerton Hotel in New York, they looked forward to the standards that have come to be expected from (1) <u>the world's fastest-grown hotel chain</u>. The hotel's website promises (2) <u>a welcoming atmosphere</u>, a good range of (3) <u>provided boutique shops on-site</u>, and health and safety standards exceeding (4) <u>those by law required</u>. However, within 48 hours of the hotel's grand opening, the first 180 guests had experienced:
>
> - Theft – over $20000 of (5) <u>personal possessions stolen</u> were found in a waiter's accommodation.
> - Unexpected extra charges – many guests found themselves being asked to pay for (6) <u>items included</u> at no extra cost in most hotels – such as (7) <u>used towels</u>.
> - Cold – a (8) <u>broken heating system</u> was blamed for temperatures as low as –2° inside the hotel.
> - Fear – several guests experienced a (9) <u>raising-hair ride</u> in an elevator that descended more than 50 floors without stopping.
>
> Over 100 guests checked out after a single night. (10) <u>Those remained</u> were keen to talk to our reporter. 'I reckon the New York Shallerton is just one big (11) <u>money-making</u> exercise,' said one (12) <u>suffering long guest</u>.

1	....	7	....
2	....	8	....
3	....	9	....
4	....	10	....
5	....	11	....
6	....	12	....

116 The problems at the hotel are reported on local radio, and more guests are interviewed. Fill each gap using the verb in brackets in an appropriate form and adding words as necessary.

'We were ready (1) ......*to spend*...... (spend) a really relaxing weekend in New York, but ended up feeling inclined (2) .... (sue) the company – it made us really mad! I was just astonished (3) .... (have) the nerve to put fresh towels on my bill. I have to say that we were shocked (4) .... (not provide) better service. It's such a shame – the hotel was lovely and new. We could see that the staff felt awkward (5) .... (admit) the problems they were having, and it wasn't their fault – it was nice (6) .... (see) some of them really making an effort, given the circumstances.'

'We were busy (7) .... (hold) a small meeting in the hotel when we became aware (8) .... (get) colder and colder. We weren't sure (9) .... (happen), but pretty soon it became clear that it would be crazy (10) .... (go on). It was so annoying (11) .... (be told) that we couldn't complete our meeting, and I can't help feeling that it was unprofessional (12) .... (not check) everything was ready before opening for business. We don't feel at all guilty (13) .... (ask) for our money back!'

117 In these texts, risk–takers in very different fields talk about their attitudes to risk. Use the adjectives provided to fill the gaps.

alike	chemical	complete	pure	rash	similar

Simon Woodroffe, entrepreneur

I'd spent 20 years in the entertainment business before I opened the first Yo! (sushi restaurant) in London in 1997. I had just come out of a divorce, had no money, no future, was in my 40s, felt like a (1) .... failure and thought – this is it. I may have missed the boat. It was a moment of (2) .... desperation. I talk to other (3) .... entrepreneurs and we're all (4) .... ; it was a moment of desperation, or they deliberately put themselves in such a position by making (5) .... commitments so that they have to fight to keep going. In business I like to push a little further each time – I suppose it's an addiction. Perhaps risk-taking is all about a (6) .... imbalance .

afraid	alone	minimum	quick	sheer	tough

Jeremy Thompson, Sky News War reporter

I came up through journalism the traditional way, so I was in my 30s when I started getting the (7) .... assignments and had become capable of making risk assessments with the (8) .... delay. Your first impulse is to get the story and – in these days of 24-hour news – you have to get it quicker and better than the other guy. Survival is about (9) .... instinct and an ability to make (10) .... decisions.

I certainly don't think I'm a hero, but my wife told me to tell you that I went white-water rafting for my last holiday. She thinks I'm an adrenalin junkie. The truth is, you need to feel (11) .... to stay alive. It always helps to have a team around you – the photographers who go out (12) .... are most often the ones who don't come back.

118   Imagine some more things that the reporter and his wife might say looking back on his time as a war reporter. Use the words in the circles in a suitable order to make complete sentences. The first word of each sentence has been given to help you.

1   (good   see   danger zone   my   articles   newspaper)

It *was always good to see my danger zone articles in the newspaper.*

2   (was   operator   often   liked   lone   but   that way)

I ....

3   (prefer   journalist   good   remember   absolutely   one   pretty   than   perfect)

I'd ....

4   (dangerous   those places   want   go   but   to)

Going ....

5   (older   decision   safer   got   conscious   trips)

As ....

6   (make   danger zone   husband   nervous   me   know)

Knowing ....

119   In these short dialogues, cross out any options that are unlikely or not possible.

"

a   A: People are terribly worried about this new shopping centre development. The building works caused flooding again last week.

   B: Really? Why's that?

   A: The (1) underlying cause / ~~the cause underlying~~ seems to be a stream they've diverted to make the foundations.

   B: They'll have to cancel the whole thing, won't they?

   A: It's (2) the only solution possible / one possible solution / one solution possible as far as I can see. A lot of (3) concerned people / the people concerned are protesting in the square tomorrow morning. I think I'll go along.

b   A: There's Ethan Hawke, getting out of that limousine!

   B: It's funny, a magazine article I read said he was (4) very unheard of / almost unheard of / rather unpopular, but look how many people have turned out to see him!

c   A: I thought that was (5) <u>very wonderful / very good / really wonderful</u>, didn't you? Ethan
       Hawke's role is (6) <u>almost unique / rather unusual / utterly unusual</u>.
    B: I don't agree, I'm afraid. I felt it was (7) <u>hugely disappointing / totally disappointing / simply
       awful</u>. Too many special effects and not enough of a story.

d   A: It's (8) <u>lovely and sunny / nice and warm / nice and bright</u> today, isn't it? Let's sit outside.
    B: That would be nice – I haven't seen your garden for ages.
    A: So what do you think?
    B: It's (9) <u>extremely lovely / perfectly lovely</u>! You've taken down some trees at the end, haven't you?
    A: Yes. I wanted (10) <u>the light to be maximum / maximum light</u> in that part of the garden.

20A   Which of these statements do you agree with? Decide what the difference in meaning is
between the underlined pairs of adjectives. Then add the adverb *very* before any of the
adjectives that you can.

1   a <u>Wild</u> animals should not be kept in captivity.
    b People who have a <u>wild</u> social life are usually unhappy underneath.

2   a Most governments are prepared to respond to <u>public</u> opinion.
    b Celebrities who lead a <u>public</u> life quickly become less interesting.

3   a Watching too much TV can lead to <u>odd</u> behaviour.
    b Wearing <u>odd</u> socks is a sign of originality.

4   a <u>French</u> bread is the best in the world.
    b Having a glass of wine at lunchtime is a <u>French</u> habit which some consider unhealthy.

5   a Children should be encouraged to behave in an <u>adult</u> way from an early age.
    b The <u>adult</u> population of the country numbers over 10 million.

6   a Many <u>old</u> people are right when they claim that standards of respect are falling.
    b You can never really be friends with an <u>old</u> boyfriend or girlfriend.

20B   Now write your own pairs of statements using these adjectives, firstly in a non-gradable
sense, then in a gradable sense.

critical

....

....

average

....

....

genuine

....

....

Comparatives and superlatives
(comparative and superlative forms, phrases and clauses)

121 Rewrite these sentences using the words in brackets. Your rewritten sentences should have the same meaning as the originals.

1 We're often told that girls are so much better at reading than boys in a way that suggests this is a new phenomenon. (worse)
We're often told that boys are so much worse at reading than girls.

2 In the mid-1970s, academics thought they had discovered why boys were worse at reading than girls. (good)

3 Apparently, girls tend to socialise earlier than boys, who are more inclined to introspective activities. (later / not as)

4 Boys, on the other hand, are more interested in doing something creative. (less)

5 Boys also tend to read more slowly than girls. (as quickly)

6 Educationalists are not as concerned as parents about this phenomenon. (more)

7 Some researchers believe that boys' methodical approach to a text explains why they prefer non-fiction, as their mentality is better suited to understanding information than feelings. (well-suited)

122 Look at the underlined sections in these short conversations. Correct any errors. If the section is correct, write ✓.

a A: So, how was the holiday?
  B: (1) <u>It was OK, but it wasn't as quite as comfortable a hotel as we'd expected.</u>
  A: And the weather?
  B: (2) The weather was perfect. Maybe 'perfect' is not the right word. <u>In fact, one day it was absolutely blistering – much hot for us.</u>
  A: What about the food?
  B: Terrible. (3) <u>Most of the time it was so too overcooked that it was inedible.</u>

b A: Did you enjoy the play?
  B: (4) <u>No, I'm afraid not. We got to the theatre too late to get in.</u>
  A: So what did you do?
  B: We went to the cinema. (5) <u>At least it wasn't expensive as the theatre.</u>

c A: The tennis was disappointing, wasn't it? I really wanted Henstock to win.
  B: (6) <u>Yes, but he just didn't play as well enough, did he?</u>

A: (7) <u>No, Ruddock was certainly best player on the day.</u>

B: (8) <u>The truth is that Henstock is not a good player as Ruddock.</u>

d A: (9) <u>I didn't think I'd enjoy the food at that restaurant, but I couldn't have been wrong.</u>

B: What did you have?

A: (10) I had seafood. <u>It was the tastiest fish than I've ever eaten.</u>

e A: Did you enjoy the exhibition at the weekend.

B: Yes, I did. (11) <u>I thought some of the sculptures were most unusual.</u>

f A: Did you get the exam grade you needed to get to university?

B: No, unfortunately not. I missed it by half a grade.

A: (12) <u>How a high grade did you need to get?</u>

B I needed 7.5 and I only got 7.0.

1	....	7	....
2	....	8	....
3	....	9	....
4	....	10	....
5	....	11	....
6	....	12	....

123 **Which sets of sentences have a similar meaning?**

1 a The clothes she wears for work are most unusual.

 b These are the most unusual clothes I've seen her wearing for work.

2 a I'd say she was more lucky than clever to have got that job.

 b She was very lucky to get that job because she's not very clever.

 c She wasn't so much clever as lucky to have got that job.

3 a She's not old enough to go to university.

 b She's too young to go to university.

4 a The job was not so difficult as I'd expected.

 b The job was not as difficult as I'd expected.

 c The job was less difficult than I'd expected.

5 a He didn't perform well enough at the interview to be given the job.

 b He didn't perform sufficiently well at the interview to be given the job.

6 a Of all the students in the class, Maria is the brightest.

 b Maria is brighter than all the other students in the class.

 c Maria is the brightest student in the class.

7 a Last winter was cold, but this winter is even more cold.

 b This winter is colder than last winter.

 c Last winter was not as cold as this winter.

124 Look at the adverbs and adverb phrases which are underlined in this newspaper story. In the spaces below, write any alternative positions where these words and phrases could be written. In some cases, no other position is possible.

Late pupils face exclusion

A 15-year-old schoolboy is being threatened with exclusion from school after arriving (1) <u>just one minute late</u> for morning lessons.

Tim Appleyard, who was delayed by an overdue bus, walked out of school (2) <u>angrily</u> after being given a detention for his late arrival. It is not unusual for this particular bus to be late arriving at the school, but on previous occasions this has been accepted by the school. The boy is refusing to accept his punishment even though this may (3) <u>eventually</u> lead to his exclusion from the school.

(4) <u>This morning</u> the headteacher of the school said in an interview that the boy only had himself to blame. He said it was the responsibility of all students to ensure they arrived at school (5) <u>on time</u> and he stressed that the boy should have caught an earlier bus to make sure he arrived (6) <u>promptly</u>.

The boy's parents have (7) <u>severely</u> criticised the school for their rigidity.

His mother said (8) <u>furiously</u>: 'We are (9) <u>completely</u> amazed by the school's inflexible attitude. Staff (10) <u>really</u> should spend more time on important issues like teaching. Tim is a hard-working student who loves school. He has never missed school (11) <u>deliberately</u>.'

---

1 ...for morning lessons just one minute late.

2 ....

3 ....

4 ....

5 ....

6 ....

7 ....

8 ....

9 ....

10 ....

11 ....

---

125 Choose the more natural words or phrases in these short conversations.

a A: I'm (1) <u>real / really</u> sorry for what I said.

   B: It's OK now, but I was (2) <u>deep / deeply</u> hurt at the time.

b A: Were you expecting a visit from your brother and his family?

   B: No, not at all. They just dropped in (3) <u>unexpectedly / in an unexpected way</u>.

c   A: I've (4) <u>just / justly</u> phoned Tom on his mobile.

    B: Did he say where he was?

    A: No, he (5) <u>flat / flatly</u> refused to tell me.

d   A: Have you noticed Joseph behaving strangely recently? I think he's up to something.

    B: Why do you say that?

    A: Well, when I came into the room, he (6) <u>quick / quickly</u> put the phone down.

e   A: You were very brave to say what you did. Everybody agrees but nobody dares to speak.

    B: I know that, but even I stopped (7) <u>short / shortly</u> of saying what I really think.

f   PATIENT: One of my back teeth is really aching.

    DENTIST: OK. If you could open your mouth (8) <u>wide / widely</u>, I'll be able to see if there's a problem there.

g   A: How's Max? I haven't seen him (9) <u>late / lately</u>.

    B: He's in America at the moment. Actually, he phoned the other day to say he's coming to see us (10) <u>direct / directly</u> he gets back to this country.

h   A: Did you see that bird?

    B: No. What was it doing?

    A: It was hovering (11) <u>high / highly</u> above the field, presumably looking for food.

126 Add the adverbs or adverb phrases in brackets to these sentences. Mark the position with ▲. Some adverbs or phrases may go in more than one position.

1   Motorists who drive illegally are being caught and fined thanks to the introduction of new number plate readers. (automatically)

2   Traffic police are using these readers to check computer records. (regularly)

3   They let officers know whether vehicles are taxed and insured, or whether drivers are wanted for other offences. (immediately)

4   Since the technology was introduced the team have made more than 1,000 arrests for driving and criminal offences. (three years ago)

5   The police inspector who leads the project, said... (currently)

6   'Untaxed vehicles, road safety offences and crime are linked.' (clearly)

7   'Our new system seems to be working as a way of catching people who shouldn't be on our roads.' (very efficiently)

1   <u>Motorists who drive illegally are being caught and fined ▲ thanks to the introduction of new number plate readers.</u>

2   ....

3   ....

4   ....

5   ....

6   ....

7   ....

127   Look at this short story. Correct the errors or make improvements related to the form and/or the position of the underlined adverbs and adverb phrases. Write ✓ if the adverb is used correctly.

Man v Coat

The first and only time we met (1) <u>in an upstairs bar</u> was on a cold November night. I'd answered (2) <u>excitedly</u> the ad she'd put in the local paper. '...would like to meet a self-assured man in his mid-thirties, a man who likes walks in the park and talks in the dark.' There was a simple quality to her writing that (3) <u>greatly</u> had appealed to me.

She was a tall slender brunette in her mid-thirties. She was both pretty and smart and I liked her (4) <u>immediately</u>. I decided straightaway that I wanted to (5) <u>definitely</u> see her again. Even better, she seemed (6) <u>equally</u> keen to see me again. If only I (7) <u>successfully</u> could manage the rest of the evening without making a mistake.

As we got ready to leave, she was first to put on her coat. Once ready, she stood there, (8) <u>patiently</u> waiting for me. I took my coat from the back of the chair and, gripping (9) <u>firmly</u> the collar with my left hand, put my right arm into the right sleeve. With the coat half on, I stretched (10) <u>backwards</u> my left arm to catch the left sleeve. Somehow I couldn't find it, so I tried again and missed (11) <u>once more</u>.

Absorbed in what I was doing (12) <u>completely</u>, I didn't notice that my body was beginning to move (13) <u>undignifiedly</u> in an anti-clockwise direction. As I twisted (14) <u>clumsily</u>, the coat twisted too; the sleeve remained (15) <u>in a stubborn fashion</u> the same distance from my hand. I could feel sweat beginning to break out on my forehead. It was as if the sleeves had grown (16) <u>more closely</u> together while we'd been in the bar. I grunted and groaned (17) <u>loud</u> as I struggled to gain the upper hand, or more (18) <u>accurate</u> perhaps, the upper sleeve.

No man can remain standing while (19) <u>madly</u> twisting and stabbing at a (20) <u>fastly</u> moving sleeve. I began to lose my balance. (21) <u>Slowly</u> I sank to the ground. Lying there in a heap with my coat covering (22) <u>partially</u> me, I glanced up at my companion. Neither of us said a word. Never before had she seen a man wrestled to the ground by his own coat (23) <u>so aggressively</u>.

Adverbs 2
(degree and focus adverbs; comment and viewpoint adverbs;
adverbial clauses of time; adverbs of place, direction, frequency, time)

Units 74–79

128 Choose the more natural words or phrases in these short conversations. Sometimes both options are appropriate.

a   A: Where are you going?
    B: I'm going inside. It's (1) <u>too / very</u> cold to stay outside without a coat.

b   A: Have you seen Ed?
    B: Yes, briefly, but he'd hardly been in two minutes (2) <u>before / than</u> he went out again.

c   A: I've got to be in London by 8.30. I hope I don't miss my train.
    B: Don't worry. At this time of the day, trains (3) <u>hourly leave to Madrid / to Madrid leave hourly</u>.

d   A: Did you like the film better than the book?
    B: No, I didn't. In fact, I (4) <u>much / very much</u> prefer reading to going to the cinema.

e   A: Are you settled in your new flat now?
    B: Yes, thanks – and thanks for all your help, it was (5) <u>much / very</u> appreciated.

f   A: Eleanor's looking tired again – and it's only Monday.
    B: She (6) <u>almost always looks tired / looks almost always tired</u> after the weekend.

g   A: Mario said he was (7) <u>much / very</u> fed up with his job, but he still hasn't given in his notice.
    B: I know, but (8) <u>alone he / he alone</u> can make that decision.

h   A: Isn't it time you went to college?
    B: Yes, but I'm not leaving (9) <u>before / until</u> the post comes.

i   A: So you weren't hurt in the accident?
    B: No, in fact only later (10) <u>did I realise / I realised</u> how lucky I'd been.

129 Explain the difference in meaning, if any, between these sets of sentences.

1   a Simon feeds only the birds in the winter.
    b Only Simon feeds the birds in the winter.
    c Simon feeds the birds only in the winter.
    d Only in the winter does Simon feed the birds.

2   a Unusually, she was early for her appointment.
    b She was unusually early for her appointment.

3   a I sincerely believe he meant what he said.
    b I believe he sincerely meant what he said.

4   a As the sun goes down, you can feel the temperature dropping.
    b When the sun goes down, you can feel the temperature dropping.

5   a Medically speaking, there's nothing wrong with her.
    b From a medical point of view, there's nothing wrong with her.
    c In medical terms, there's nothing wrong with her.

91

130 Add the adverbs or adverb phrases in brackets to these sentences. Mark the position with ▲. Some adverbs or phrases may go in more than one position. You may have to change the word order of the sentences.

1 A businessman had an important meeting that involved his flying from London to New York. (one day last week)

2 When he left home in the morning, his wife drove him and accompanied him to the check-in. (to the airport)

3 She waved him goodbye he went through Passport Control. (then / as)

4 She did some shopping and returned to the car. (at the airport shops)

5 She was getting into her car her husband's plane was taking off. (as)

6 His flight from London to New York was direct. (naturally)

7 He reached New York, he went directly through Immigration and Customs. (when)

8 He had no baggage to collect as he had taken a briefcase for his short trip. (only)

9 He went through to the Arrivals Hall and his wife was there to greet him. (incredibly)

10 It was that morning that she had seen him off. (only)

11 She had travelled by plane or boarded a ship. (at no time during the day)

12 The question is this: how could the man's wife have met him? (at the airport)

31A Complete this urban myth[1], filling the gaps with the most likely adverbs and phrases from the box.

> astonishingly   from outside their house   from work   gratefully   later the same day
> neatly   one morning   promptly   the following weekend   the next weekend   too
> urgently   very   when

A young couple woke up
(1) .... to find
that their car had been stolen
(2) .... They
(3) .... phoned
the police and reported the theft
before leaving for work.
(4) ....
they returned home
(5) .... to find
the car back again in the usual
place. There was also an envelope
(6) .... placed under the windscreen wiper. Inside was a
(7) .... polite note of apology. The writer explained that he had borrowed
the car because his wife was having a baby and he'd had to take her to the hospital
(8) .... To make up for this, there were also two free tickets to a big rock
concert (9) .... The young couple weren't (10) .... angry
and accepted the tickets (11) ....

(12) .... they went to the concert, but (13) .... they got
home afterwards, they found that the polite thief had taken advantage of their absence and
robbed their house of its contents. (14) ...., they also found out from the
police that their car had been used for another robbery on the day it had disappeared.

31B Rewrite the first paragraph of the story, putting the adverbs and adverb phrases in alternative places in the sentences. Some adverbs cannot change place.

---

[1]*Urban myths* are well-known stories that many people believe to be true, but which, in actual fact, may be greatly exaggerated or made-up.

Conjunctions
(reason, purpose, result and contrast)

132 Jo has emailed her neighbour Kate to ask her to look after her house while she is away. Use the conjunctions to complete the email. Sometimes more than one conjunction is possible.

seeing as   since   so as not to   so (that)   though   to   while   with

Kate

Thanks so much for your offer to keep an eye on the house. (1) *Since / Seeing as* Mum's quite unwell, I'm not exactly sure when I'll be back, but I'd be so grateful if you could pop in every couple of days (2) .... the plants get watered and you can check that everything's all right. A few things you need to know:

The front door locks can be a bit tricky, (3) .... you need to turn the key and handle at the same time. (4) .... you're only next door, I'd rather keep the alarm set – the code is 5512, as you know – and when you go out again press 'yes' after you enter the code (5) .... it sets itself properly.

I've left the lamp in the hall on a timer switch. If you need to turn on a light, use a different one (6) .... disturb the timer settings. It might be a good idea to draw different curtains each time you go in, (7) .... make it look like the house is occupied.

My mobile number is 06677 312464 – I won't have it on when I'm visiting Mum in hospital, (8) ....

Thanks again Kate. (9) .... so many things to sort out, I doubt I'll be back before the weekend, but hope to see you then.

Jo

133 A manager is talking to staff about the security of an office building. Rewrite the underlined sections in a less formal style.

Thanks everyone for coming. This is a rather unusual meeting (1) <u>in that</u> I've called it with so little notice, but I'd like to draw your attention to a matter of concern. (2) <u>Whilst</u> I don't want to focus on negative issues, it's better to talk about problems when they come up (3) <u>so as to be able to</u> work out the best solutions. (4) <u>Since</u> I have to go to Head Office quite often, I'm often unable to oversee the security of this building myself, and there have been a few lapses recently when I've been away. (5) <u>Whilst convinced</u> that common sense is the best guide in most circumstances, I have prepared some instructions (6) <u>such that</u> you will always know the correct procedures in my absence. I would like you to study these immediately, (7) <u>for</u> it is important that we keep up the highest standards.

1	*because*	5	....
2	....	6	....
3	....	7	....
4	....		

134 Some prize-winning scientists are talking about their achievements. Rewrite each sentence including the conjunction in brackets and making any other necessary changes.

1   We were worried that we would not be able to continue with our research because funding cuts were threatened. (since)
Since funding cuts were threatened, we were worried that we would not be able to continue with our research.

2   To make sure there was no risk of losing any data, we worked on two sites and two computer networks. (so that)

....

3   Although two valuable team members left mid-way through, we managed to meet our deadlines. (in spite of)

....

4   We were exhausted, but the final two months were the most productive of all. (though)

....

5   The whole team worked hard, so we succeeded. (due to)

....

135 Now the scientists give some details about their experiments. Match the sentence beginnings (1–8) with the endings (a–h), and fill each gap with a word or phrase from the box.

Example: _The material was quite unusual in that it was strong but extraordinarily light._

| because   due to   for   ~~in that~~   of   owing to   that   though |

1   ~~The material was quite unusual~~ .... ~~it was strong,~~ ...
2   The success of the experiment was...
3   We wondered if the colour had changed because...
4   .... the massive weight of the material, ...
5   Difficult .... the conditions were, ...
6   The plants were all the healthier ....
7   It was such a minute particle to detect...
8   .... this method hadn't been tried before, ...

a   ... . the equipment had to be extremely precise.
b   ...largely .... careful preparation.
c   ...it proved impossible to construct strong enough equipment to measure it accurately.
d   ...we managed to retrieve over 50 samples.
e   ... . exposure to fresh air and sunlight.
f   ...we were unsure how the results would come out.
g   ... . the presence of a gas.
h   ...~~but extraordinarily light.~~

136A In the 1880s, two scientists devised an experiment to test for the existence of the ether. Read the first part of this description of their experiment, and choose the correct conjunctions. Sometimes more than one option is possible.

In the 1880s, scientists believed that an invisible substance called the 'ether' filled all space. The ether was thought to be a constant 'wind', (1) <u>though / while / despite the fact that</u> all other bodies moved through it. They thought that light, (2) <u>although / despite the fact that / inasmuch as</u> it was not part of the ether, also consisted of waves travelling through the ether.

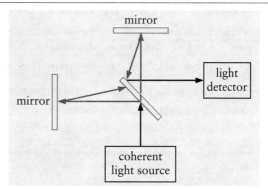

Albert Michelson and Edward Morley were American scientists who wanted to prove the existence of the ether. They used the idea that the direction of the earth's motion relative to the ether wind would differ as it moved around the sun: in one season the ether would appear to be moving in one direction, (3) <u>whereas / while / inasmuch as</u> it would seem to be moving in a different direction in another.

Michelson and Morley predicted that light would travel more quickly if it was moving in the same direction as the ether. They developed the Michelson Interferometer (4) <u>so as to / in order to / owing to</u> test their theory. It worked as follows:

A beam of light is split into two beams, one travelling one way, (5) <u>while / whereas / due to</u> the other travels in the opposite direction. The beams are reflected off mirrors, and return to the same point, (6) <u>so that / because / whilst</u> they have travelled exactly the same distance. A detector is placed at the source (7) <u>as / in such a way that / so that</u> it can record whether the beams arrive back at the same moment or not.

136B Now read the remainder of the description of the experiment, and expand the notes in brackets to fill the gaps.

If both beams take the same time to travel, they will arrive back at the detector at the same time, (1) (while / arrive) <u>while they will arrive</u> at different times if there is any difference in the time taken to travel.

(2) (Despite / fact / repeat) .... their experiment time and time again, Michelson and Morley found no difference in the time taken for the light beams to reach the detector. They even tried the experiment at different times of year, (3) (so / could / see) .... whether the position of the earth made a difference. It did not.

(4) (Primitive / though / technology) .... , Michelson and Morley made the following discoveries:

• the ether does not exist
• the speed of light in a vacuum is always the same, (5) (even) .... the positions of the light source and detector are changed.

(6) (Even) .... scientists had speculated about its existence for generations, it was the work of Michelson and Morley that put an immediate end to belief in the ether. (7) (While / intend) .... to discover the ether, the two scientists instead disproved its existence, (8) (such / that) .... our understanding of light was changed forever.

37 Choose the appropriate words or phrases in these short conversations. Sometimes both options may be correct.

"

a A: If you (1) <u>think / thought</u> someone has stolen your credit card, phone the police immediately.
   B: What (2) <u>will / would</u> happen if I don't?
   A: I'm not sure, but if I (3) <u>am / were</u> you, (4) <u>I'll / I'd</u> definitely phone the police and the credit card company.

b A: Why do you go on doing the lottery if you never (5) <u>win / won</u> anything?
   B: I don't really know. But if I (6) <u>haven't won / didn't win</u> this week, (7) <u>I'm going to stop / I'll stop</u> doing it.

c A: What's the matter, Dean?
   B: I can't decide (8) <u>if / whether</u> to go out or have an early night.
   A: Don't go out (9) <u>if you don't / unless you</u> really want to.

d A: I'm exhausted. I feel (10) <u>like if / as if</u> I haven't slept for a week.
   B: Well, if you (11) <u>will work / work</u> such long hours, what do you expect?

e A: I can't stand this hot, humid weather.
   B: Neither can I. I really wish it (12) <u>was / were</u> a bit cooler.

f A: Are we still going to the theatre tomorrow?
   B: Yes, we could go tomorrow evening, (13) <u>unless you'd / if you wouldn't</u> rather go to the afternoon performance.

g A: Congratulations on winning the gold medal.
   B: Thanks, but I wouldn't have won (14) <u>if it were / were it</u> not for the support of my family.

h A: Sorry, but I can't pay the money I owe you.
   B: That's OK – you can pay half now and half next month if that (15) <u>makes / will make</u> things easier for you.
   A: Oh thanks, but it still depends on (16) <u>if / whether</u> I get paid or not.

i A: If you (17) <u>happen / should happen</u> to see Paul, ask him to reply to my text message.
   B: OK, but I don't know (18) <u>if / whether</u> I'll see him today.

j A: Do you think it's going to rain?
   B: Yes, I do. As my grandmother used to say 'If the cows are lying down, it (19) <u>means / will mean</u> it's going to rain.'

"

138 Complete this extract from a formal speech given by the leader of Green Fingers, an environmental pressure group. Choose from the items in the box.

could   had we not   if I might   if you were   if that were to happen   imagine   I would
should   unless   we would undoubtedly   were it not for   we would   whether or not

Green Fingers

(1) .... start by thanking you for all your hard work during our recent campaign. (2) .... the thousands of unpaid volunteers like you, Green Fingers could not continue to be the powerful pressure group we have become. (3) .... any of you doubt this, you only have to look at the recent fate of the some of the other national environmental groups. (4) .... streamlined our organisation and recruited new members, (5) .... have shared that same fate.

Now, turning to the future, let me say I am fully aware that there will be some disagreement amongst members about (6) .... we should use direct action tactics in our campaign to prevent the movement of nuclear waste across the country. (7) .... to ask my personal opinion, (8) .... suggest that direct action could be very effective (9) .... , of course, it turned violent. (10) .... , it is almost certain that (11) .... lose public support. (12) .... the damage that negative publicity (13) .... do to our organisation.

139A Read this information about energy sources and complete each sentence with the appropriate beginning from the list (a–d).

Green Fingers

Future energy

(1) .... due to a growing world population, demands for higher standards of living, demands for less pollution and rapidly diminishing supplies of fossil fuels.

(2) .... to sustain its infrastructure. What would happen then? The world's entire industrialised infrastructure would collapse: agriculture, transport, waste collection, information technology, communications and many of the necessities that we take for granted.

(3) .... , we will face worldwide catastrophe.

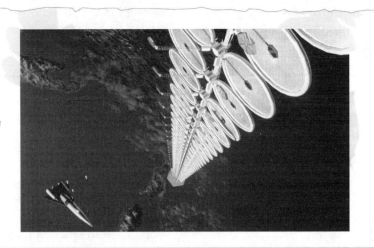

Most human energy sources today use energy from sunlight, either directly from solar cells, or in stored forms like fossil fuels. (4) .... , then the long-term energy usage of humanity would be limited to that from the sunlight falling directly on Earth.

a   Suppose the world ran seriously short of the energy needed...

b   Future energy development faces great challenges...

c   If these stored forms were used up...

d   Unless we can maintain our energy supplies...

39B   Now complete these sentences using the words given.

1   Unless humans reduce their dependence on fossil fuels, ... (global warming / serious problem)
    global warming will become a more serious problem.

2   Suppose oil and natural gas were to run out next year. (alternative energy sources?)
    ....

3   If there weren't so many cars in the world, ... (so much oil)
    ....

4   Imagine the power of the sun could be collected. (solve / energy problems)
    ....

5   Whether global warming is caused by human activity or not, ... (take seriously)
    ....

6   We're never going to solve the world's environmental problems, unless ...
    (countries / cooperate)
    ....

7   Were petrol rationing to be introduced, ... (alternative transport)
    ....

8   If it hadn't been for the invention of the petrol engine, ... (oil left)
    ....

140 Read this email from Alain who is worried because his girlfriend has told him their relationship is over. Fill the gaps with suitable words.

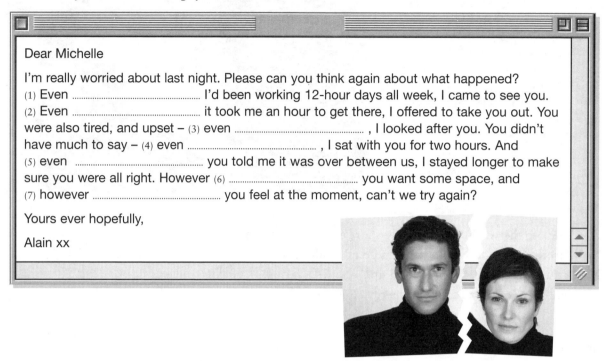

Dear Michelle

I'm really worried about last night. Please can you think again about what happened? (1) Even .... I'd been working 12-hour days all week, I came to see you. (2) Even .... it took me an hour to get there, I offered to take you out. You were also tired, and upset – (3) even .... , I looked after you. You didn't have much to say – (4) even .... , I sat with you for two hours. And (5) even .... you told me it was over between us, I stayed longer to make sure you were all right. However (6) .... you want some space, and (7) however .... you feel at the moment, can't we try again?

Yours ever hopefully,

Alain xx

141 Look at this exchange of text messages between Alain and Michelle and fill each gap using an appropriate sentence connector or conjunction from the box. There are more items in the box than you need.

anyway	as well	before that	if not	if so	in any case
likewise	provided that	so long as	too	unless	

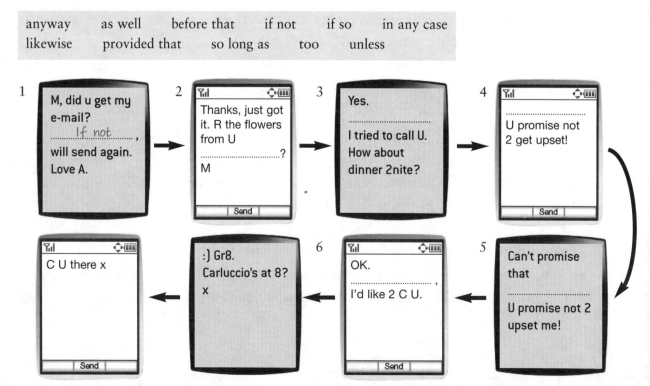

1. M, did u get my e-mail? ......If not...... , will send again. Love A.

2. Thanks, just got it. R the flowers from U ....? M

3. Yes. .... I tried to call U. How about dinner 2nite?

4. .... U promise not 2 get upset!

5. Can't promise that .... U promise not 2 upset me!

6. OK. .... , I'd like 2 C U.

:) Gr8. Carluccio's at 8? x

C U there x

142 Look at these three paragraphs about early transport. Reconstruct the paragraphs by putting the sentences in the correct order and using sentence connectors from the box to provide links.

1

at the same time   before long

People have dragged heavy objects, such as the bodies of hunted animals, along the ground from the beginning of human history.

a   Early humans realised that using 'runners' made from smooth wood made dragging much easier, especially over snow and ice, and the sledge had been invented.

b   Hunting techniques improved, and human communities started to prosper.

....

....

2

even so   and hence   however

The first wheels to be invented were heavy, being made of solid wood.

a   They allowed people and animals to move much greater weights more efficiently than before.

b   The invention of wheels with spokes, which were much lighter and allowed much faster travel.

c   Early carts could only travel at three or four kilometres per hour.

....

....

....

3

| as a result | in addition | nevertheless |

Roman roads required enormous quantities of material, and a huge workforce, to complete.

a   Individual Roman soldiers did not always praise the engineers as they toiled up a hillside.

b   The new roads enabled soldiers to travel quickly over long distances, and many of the roads were so well made that they lasted hundreds or even thousands of years.

c   They went forward in almost straight lines, and had very steep sections up and down hills.

....

....

....

143   **Use your own ideas to complete these short dialogues.**

1   A: When we go out later, let's get a taxi.
    B: Or there's a bus service that runs until late, isn't there? ....

2   A: What an amazing little car – I thought you liked big cars?
    B: I do, but they use a lot of fuel. However, ...

3   A: We're nearly home – I'm starving.
    B: Me too. As soon as we get there, ...

4   A: Here are the last two suitcases.
    B: I'm afraid the boot's already full. So ....

5   PASSENGER: This area is very remote, isn't it? When did regular flights start?
    TOUR GUIDE: Not until the 1990s. Previously ....

6   A: Can you drive for a while?
    B: Do you mind if I don't? I'm exhausted. Besides, ...

7   A: It was a shame we were too late for the film, wasn't it?
    B: Yes. All the same, ...

8   A: I don't want a meal out. I'm not hungry.
    B: Well, ... instead?

9   A: It was strange that she didn't invite us, don't you think?
    B: Yes. After all, ...

144 Complete this story by choosing the best prepositions from the box. You can use some prepositions more than once.

across	along	among	between	over	through

The helpful detective

The Waldorf Astoria is (1) .... the grandest hotels in New York and has on its staff, (2) .... with other security personnel, several detectives whose job it is to protect the wealthy hotel residents. One night a hotel detective saw a man with a suitcase trip and fall as he walked (3) .... the lobby. The suitcase hit the floor, burst open and spilled out diamonds and other jewels all (4) .... the floor. A porter joined the detective and the two men crawled on their hands and knees (5) .... the lobby picking up the jewels. (6) .... them they managed to collect them all in less than ten minutes. Then the porter called a taxi for the unfortunate guest. It was only half an hour later that the theft of over a million dollars' worth of jewellery was reported to the hotel reception.

145 Look at the the underlined prepositions in this story. Correct any errors. If the preposition is used correctly, write ✓.

A woman was being chased (1) <u>along</u> a forest by a gang of bandits. The bandits wanted to kill the woman and take two golden balls she was carrying. She ran (2) <u>between</u> a narrow track until she came to a wooden bridge which went (3) <u>through</u> a deep ravine. There was a big notice (4) <u>above</u> the bridge, which said: 'Maximum weight on this bridge 112 pounds'. The woman weighed 100 pounds and the golden balls weighed 10 pounds each. There was no time for her to get (5) <u>along</u> the bridge and come back for one of the balls later, but despite this she managed to escape (6) <u>between</u> the ravine with both balls. How was this possible?

1	....	4	....
2	....	5	....
3	....	6	....

146   Choose the correct words or phrases in these short conversations. Sometimes both alternatives may be correct.

a   A: Excuse me can you tell me how to get to the town centre?
    B: Sure. Go straight (1) <u>along / through</u> this road until you come to the park gate. Go (2) <u>along / through</u> the gate then turn down the first footpath on the right. Walk (3) <u>along / through</u> the path, right (4) <u>across / through</u> the park. Go straight on for a few hundred metres then take the subway that goes (5) <u>under / below</u> the main road. That will bring you out into the town centre.

b   A: Did you see that?
    B: What?
    A: A deer jumped (6) <u>above / over</u> the hedge on the left and ran straight (7) <u>across / through</u> the road into that field on the right.

c   A: Do you ever fall out with your flatmates?
    B: We sometimes argue over who does what. Yesterday there was a row (8) <u>among / between</u> Anna and Tom over whose turn it was to do the shopping.

d   A: Have you decided where you are going on holiday yet?
    B: No, we can't choose (9) <u>among / between</u> Italy, Spain and Greece.

e   A: Do you know what's happened to Caroline? I haven't see her recently.
    B: (10) <u>Among / Between</u> you and me, I think she's been made redundant.

f   A: Have you ever been to Ireland?
    B: Yes, several times. I love the people. They're (11) <u>among / between</u> the friendliest people in the world.

g   A: Did you see that programme on TV last night about education?
    B: No, was it interesting?
    A: Yes, it was. They were claiming that there is no definite link (12) <u>with / between</u> intelligence and exam results.

h   A: Mark always seems incredibly busy.
    B: Yes, (13) <u>among / between</u> other things, he's got five children to look after, plays in a band, writes books and has a full-time job.

47 Answer the questions with items from the box.

> a doctor   a prisoner escaping from a high security jail   a helicopter   an experienced politician
> people with sensitive or secret information   a university graduate
> someone watching a horror film   someone who has lost their door key   someone with flu

Who or what...

1   ...might have three successful election campaigns *under their belt*?
2   ...can take off vertically and then hover *above the ground*?
3   ...might feel *under par*?
4   ...might put their hands *over their eyes*?
5   ...might climb *through a window*?
6   ...might want to keep something *between themselves*?
7   ...might point to the *correlation between diet and health*?
8   ...might climb *over a high wall*?
9   ...might consider stacking shelves in a supermarket *beneath them*?

48 Use your own ideas to find possible questions for these answers.

1   Where's the cat hiding?   ?
Under the duvet.

2   ....   ?
All over the world.

3   ....   ?
He went completely over the top.

4   ....   ?
That's between me and my sister.

5   ....   ?
Right between the eyes.

6   ....   ?
Throughout America, and in many other parts of the world.

7   ....   ?
Under the sea.

8   ....   ?
Above the clouds.

149 Read this transcript of a radio news broadcast and write alternatives for each preposition or phrase in italics. Sometimes no alternative is possible.

...and now it's time for the news at five o'clock, with Lillian Tailforth.

Good evening. Here are the headlines at 5 o'clock.

The annual G8 summit has been taking place in the Spanish capital, Madrid. (1) *During* the three days of talks, world leaders will be discussing the environment and peace in the Middle East. It is not known what has been discussed (2) *so far today*, but a press conference is expected (3) *in* the next hour. General agreement is expected among the member states, (4) *except for* likely resistance to environmental initiatives from the USA.

A small bomb has exploded harmlessly in the centre of Manchester. Police say that the city has been calm (5) *until* now, and it is unclear who placed the device there.

The Hollywood actor Gene King died peacefully today at his mansion outside Los Angeles. He was 85. (6) *In* a long and distinguished career King appeared in over 30 films, winning an Oscar for his 1976 performance in The Emperor. (7) *Apart from* King, only one other American actor has won awards on four continents. His appearances had become rarer (8) *over* recent years, but he managed to record a regular weekly radio programme right (9) *up to* his final brief illness. Fans have been gathering outside his home (10) *over* the last few hours to pay their respects.

Sport: Liverpool pulled off a shock result by defeating Manchester United this afternoon. (11) *Throughout* the first half Manchester United led 1–0, but a flurry of second half goals saw Liverpool take the match 3–1.

And finally, some news of our own. This is proving to be Radio Meridian's best year (12) *to date*, with over 300,000 listeners tuning in every day. (13) *Besides* our public broadcasts, we now reach more than 6,000 patients via hospital radio. We're aiming to reach half a million listeners (14) *by* the end of the year – thank you for your support and keep listening!

1	In / Over / Throughout	8	
2		9	
3		10	
4		11	
5		12	
6		13	
7		14	

150   Complete the interview using items from the box to fill the gaps.

apart from	aside	but	by	during	except for
except that	so far	throughout	~~until~~	up till	

INTERVIEWER: So, tell me, what attracted you to this job?

CANDIDATE: Well, (1) ....*until*............ very recently, I've been trying to find work in the restaurant business, but I felt that I had more to offer.

INTERVIEWER: How do you mean?

CANDIDATE: Well, holiday jobs (2) .... , I've actually mostly had experience in the entertainment industry.

INTERVIEWER: Can you give me some examples?

CANDIDATE: Yes, I can. (3) .... my stay in Malaysia, I ran a small music venue, putting on bands and entertainment acts in a holiday resort.

INTERVIEWER: Ah yes, you spent two years in Malaysia and Indonesia. (4) .... this period, what did you find most challenging?

CANDIDATE: Probably the week I ran a nightclub on a cruise ship for wealthy tourists. That was nothing (5) .... trouble, and I would have left, (6) .... there's nowhere to go on a ship at sea!

INTERVIEWER: Which other parts of the world have you visited?

CANDIDATE: I've been to most parts of South America, (7) .... the far south of Argentina and Brazil.

INTERVIEWER: (8) .... food, which you mention here, what are your interests?

CANDIDATE: Travel, obviously, and (9) .... recently playing the guitar, but I don't get much time for that these days.

INTERVIEWER: And (10) .... you haven't had any specific experience of nightclub management in this country?

CANDIDATE: No, but it's something I'd like to achieve (11) .... the time I'm 30.

151   Answer these possible interview questions about yourself using the phrase in brackets if you can.

1   What have you been doing over the last few years? (until)

....

2   Tell me about something challenging you've experienced in your work or personal life. (during)

....

3   What's been the biggest change in your life in the last 12 months, and why? (up to)

....

4   What do you hope to be doing in a few years' time? (by)

....

5   Tell me about an experience in your life that you didn't enjoy? (except)

....

6   What about travel – have you visited many countries? (apart from)

....

152 Read this article about a famous photographer, Henri Cartier-Bresson. Put items (a–j) in the correct places in the text, adding the prepositions after the verbs.

There are very, very few photographers who are (1) .... h .... , but Henri-Cartier Bresson was one. His painterly eye for texture and composition was evident in his first photographs, taken in Africa in 1931. Each one is perfectly (2) .... , requiring no cropping or alteration.

Cartier-Bresson refused to stage photographs, instead patiently (3) .... the 'decisive moment' of unexpected drama. (4) .... of athletes and racing cars in motion, and (5) .... Leica camera, he invented a new kind of photography that was completely spontaneous, and created beautiful compositions.

He was (6) .... , and he soon met and (7) .... surrealist painters such as Picasso and Matisse. He felt he could use photography to (8) .... everyday objects and scenes.

His range of activity was huge. He (9) .... and was a portrait photographer of great insight. The great Frenchman (10) .... his death in 2004, aged 96.

a became friends ....
b collaborated .... several filmmakers
c equipped .... a then-revolutionary lightweight
d framed .... the camera's eye
e influenced .... surrealism
f Inspired .... other photographers' images
g reveal the beauty ....
h thought .... of .... primarily as fine artists
i waiting .... what he called
j went .... working until

153 Choose the correct alternatives in these extracts from school reports. Sometimes both alternatives are possible.

During the last year, I have seen tremendous (1) <u>improvements in / improvements of</u> the quality of your written work. You have every right to (2) <u>be proud in / be proud of</u> your achievements. Your (3) <u>determination to succeed / determination of succeeding</u> has paid off, and your (4) <u>desire of doing / desire to do</u> well gives you the (5) <u>chance of attaining / chance to attain</u> a place in a very good university.

I continue to feel complete (6) <u>amazement at / amazement on</u> your apparent (7) <u>lack with / lack of</u> any noticeable (8) <u>improvement with / improvement in</u> your studies. I see not the slightest (9) <u>prospect in / prospect of</u> you succeeding in your end-of-year examinations unless your attitude improves. Your (10) <u>failure of making / failure to make</u> the most of the opportunities available to you makes the (11) <u>possibility of having to / possibility to have to</u> resit your exams a very strong one indeed. I am not (12) <u>satisfied with / satisfied in</u> your efforts this year.

154 Read these statements made by parents about their daughter, Jane, and answer the questions.

a Match Stephen's original questions (1 and 2) with the statements a and b:
1 Is she well?
2 What's she doing?
a I saw Jane's old boyfriend Stephen, and he was asking after her.
b I saw Jane's old boyfriend Stephen, and he was asking about her.

b Which of the alternatives is correct?
3 Jane doesn't always choose the right way <u>to deal / of dealing</u> with relationships.
4 Jane has a strange way <u>to deal / of dealing</u> with relationships.

c Which sentences suggest Jane (= her) was <u>not</u> present?
5 When I met Paul he talked with her for hours.
6 When I met Paul he talked about her for hours.
7 When I met Paul he talked of her for hours.

d Match these statements (8 and 9) with the underlined sections in a and b which mean the same.
8 She'll think the same.
9 She'll do it because she's told to.
a Going to college is a much better idea. <u>I know she will agree to it.</u>
b Going to college is a much better idea. <u>I know she will agree with it.</u>

155 Read this letter from a university professor and fill each gap, choosing a verb or noun from the first box and a preposition from the second box. You will need to use some prepositions more than once.

agree discussion ~~enquiring~~ interview involved	about in of
option permission proposals sole intention talk	on to with

Dear Mr Ellison

Thank you for (1) ..... *enquiring about* ..... the possibility of a secondment[1] to this department. Before we can (2) .... a request of this nature, we would ask you to attend an (3) .... two senior members of the department, who will ask you to (4) .... aspects of your research. You will also be (5) .... a short hypothetical (6) .... the future of the department, and during this you are welcome to make (7) .... change the way the department functions.

Please be assured that these procedures are carried out with the (8) .... ensuring that both parties would be happy with a secondment, and you have the (9) .... withdrawing from the process at any stage.

If we receive, by return email, your (10) .... proceed on this basis, we will arrange a mutually convenient time for the interview.

With best regards,
Professor Michael Pottinger

156 Look at these examples of formal writing from various contexts and join each beginning (1–8) to an ending (a–h) using *of* or *to*.

Example:
The group was formed with the ambition of starting an entirely new school of painting.

1   The group was formed with the ambition
2   The talks were hampered by both parties' refusal
3   The job requires the ability
4   It is said that the artist was ashamed
5   Our client's decision
6   We have not the slightest intention
7   The atmosphere in the house was odd, and I had a distinct sense

a   communicate effectively in many diverse situations.
b   negotiate openly with each other.
c   being unwelcome.
d   his later works and refused to display them.
e   ~~starting an entirely new school of painting.~~
f   submitting to their demands.
g   approach the committee himself was unwise.

[1]*secondment* = a period of time you spend away from your usual job in order to study or to do another job

110

57 Complete these short conversations using the words in brackets.

"

a A: Laura's nothing like her mother, is she?
 B: No, she (1) <u>takes after her father</u> . (her father / take after)

b A: Let me know if you want me to help you to (2) .... (the party arrangements / sort out)
 B: Thanks. I might well (3) .... (your offer / take up on)

c A: I'm sorry, but I've heard it all before. These are just excuses.
 B: It's different this time. Please, (4) .... (me / hear out)

d A: Have you seen Elaine recently?
 B: It's funny you should ask. I (5) .... in town yesterday. (her / run into)

e A: Who was that on the phone?
 B: Tony. I told him to (6) .... this afternoon. (me / call back)

f A: Could I ask you a favour?
 B: Of course.
 A: Could you (7) .... these shoes – they're incredibly tight. (me / help off with)

g A: I wish I could (8) .... borrowing so much money from the bank. (my brother / talk out of)
 B: What does he need it for?
 A: He's trying to (9) .... (one of his business rivals / take over)

h A: Are you sure you know what to do?
 B: Not really. Could you (10) .... once more, please? (it / go over)

i A: When do you think the next election will be?
 B: I think it'll be fairly soon – the government has (11) .... recently. (a lot of criticism / come in for)
 A: Yes, it has. But the president's still very popular, isn't he?
 B: Yes, I think that's because people (12) .... as a kind of role model. (him / look up to)

j A: You look exhausted. What have you been doing?
 B: I've been (13) .... all morning. (the garage / cleaning up)
 I've (14) .... that we don't need. (lots of things / throw away)

"

158 Complete these pairs of sentences with the appropriate forms of phrasal verbs from the box.

| break in | cut out | hold out | look up | look out | pick up | split up | ~~turn up~~ |

1 a .... *Turn up* .... the volume can you – I can't make out what they're saying!
  b Seventy thousand people .... *turned up* .... to see the first international match of the season.

2 a The strike lasted for over a year – but the employers knew the workers couldn't .... indefinitely.
  b If you want the present I've bought you, ... your hand.

3 a My brother and his wife had only been married for a year when they ....
  b The teacher usually .... the class .... to work on their projects.

4 a We were at the cinema when the burglars ....
  b The police always .... trainees by sending them out with experienced officers.

5 a We were flying at 10,000 metres when one of the plane's engines ....
  b He saw an advert for a job in the paper, so he .... it ....

6 a I've got a dreadful cold – I think I must have .... it .... at work.
  b The film started very slowly, but .... after about half an hour.

7 a If you .... , you'll see beautiful paintings on the ceiling.
  b If you don't understand a word, ... it .... in the dictionary.

8 a If you still want to borrow that book, I'll .... it .... for you.
  b .... ! There's a car coming straight towards us.

159 A student has been asked to write a ghost story. Find and correct any errors in this extract from her story.

> was
> There ~~were~~ a door to the left and another to the right, and she went through the one
> on the left. Her eyes started to become accustomed to the darkness, and she noticed it
> how she felt cold in this room with high ceilings. There were dust in the air, lit up by
> sunlight coming through a thin gap between the curtains. There was dark, heavy furniture
> in the room, and there was tall bookcases which stood all along one wall. There were an
> old-fashioned sofa and two chairs in one corner, but she was most surprised by there
> were clocks everywhere, on every surface – there was even one or two on the arms of
> chairs – and it was clear none of them worked.

160 Use your own ideas to complete these short conversations. In each gap add a *what*-clause using the verb in brackets.

"

1 A: Why are you so late?
   B: Because my train was cancelled. So _what I did was take a bus_ (do), but that took much longer, of course.

2 A: Why was the exam so difficult?
   B: Because we thought we were going to write about economic policy, but
   .... (be asked / do) instead.

3 A: You told me you could come to my party next Saturday, didn't you?
   B: Not quite. .... (say).

4 A: You don't look very happy. What's the matter?
   B: Oh, it's my boyfriend. .... (upset).

5 A: Belated Happy Birthday! What did you do to celebrate?
   B: Well, my two best friends have just had a row. So ....
   (decide / do).

"

161 Fill each gap in these short dialogues with an *it*-clause. Use the verbs or verb phrases in the box and add any other language you need.

amaze / hear   can't / guarantee   leave / do   look   strike   transpire / take   ~~no use / give~~

1 A: Here's your tennis racket.
   B: ......*It's no use giving*.... me that now – I needed it this morning.
   A: Oh, I'm so sorry. I didn't think you'd be here today.

2 A: Did you hear that Harry has left his job?
   B: Yes, ... that.
   A: Yes, I was pretty surprised too.

3 A: Well, what do you think of my new outfit?
   B: .... great! I'm not sure about the tie though.
   A: Oh dear. It cost almost as much as the shirt!

4 A: I've got so much to do – and now I've got to go to the shops as well.
   B: Hey, don't worry! Just .... I've got plenty of time.
   A: Really? Thank you so much.

5 A: Have you had a look at the map?
   B: Well, ... that we would make faster progress by travelling cross-country.
   A: Oh really? Show me!

6 EMPLOYEE: We usually get a bonus at Christmas. I was wondering if you could tell me what the situation is this year.
   MANAGER: .... there'll be an award this year, but if sales continue to rise I'm hopeful.
   EMPLOYEE: Thank you.

7 A: What happened about that stolen painting that was in last week's news?
   B: Oh, ... by an employee, so it was easy to track down.
   A: What a relief!

162 In this dialogue a father is trying to find out about a disagreement between his two children. Fill the gaps with a *there-*, *it-*, *that-* or *what-*clause using the items in brackets to help you.

FATHER: (1) (seem / be) ...*There seems to be*.... some disagreement here. What's it all about, and who started it?

OSCAR: Well it wasn't me – (2) (Jon / who) .... started it!

JON: I hate it (3) (when / tell lies) .... (4) (started / was) .... Oscar taking my football, you know, my special one that I got for my birthday.

OSCAR: And I did that because you were trying to annoy me by playing your music so loudly, weren't you?

FATHER: Calm down you two – (5) (no need) .... to get at each other like this. Were you trying to annoy him, Jon? You must admit the music was pretty loud.

JON: Well, (6) (said / was) .... that he was better at football than me.

OSCAR: No, I didn't!

FATHER: Right, listen. I don't suppose you two will ever agree. (7) (suggest) .... is that you both try to forget about it. Come and have something to eat, and then (8) (film and a football match) .... to watch on TV this afternoon. Is it a deal?

163 Fill the gaps in this article using the items in the box.

Is there a	It's a bit difficult to	it strikes me that
It emerges	it's all	there is
it occurs to me	It's an	there were
It is said that	~~It's symmetry that~~	What I used to do

Little Things that We Do

A friend phones to tell me that each time she visits her bathroom, she feels obliged to count each tile on the bathroom floor. 'I count them in threes,' she says, 'and if some of them are covered by a rug, then I have to move it. (1) _It's symmetry that_ makes me do it,' she says, as if that explains everything. When another friend admits that she cannot sit in the theatre without counting all the spotlights in the hope that the total will be divisible by five, (2) .... there is an awful lot of counting going on.

(3) .... window or chimney or telegraph pole in the land that has not been nervously counted a thousand times? I hope not. Another friend emails me, and he might have some explaining to do. '(4) .... describe,' he writes, 'but I'll give it a go.' (5) .... that if he is distracted whilst walking towards a door, and has to make a 360-degree turn, then he has to make a reverse 360-degree turn before he can actually open the door. And a neighbour, Johnnie, as sensible a man as any who ever worked with computers, also seems to display some form of obsessive behaviour. 'I used to walk to school, and (6) .... two big monkey puzzle trees about 50 metres apart. (7) .... was hold my breath while I walked between them to make sure I grew up happy.'

Why do we carry out these little, obsessive rituals? (8) .... we are all hard-wired[1] to find visible signs of organisation in the midst of chaos. And one expert, Mark Adeney, says '(9) .... extraordinary thing. All of us at some time have had a habit that we are more attached to than we would like to admit.' And (10) .... at this point that (11) .... perhaps something Mark would like to tell me. Sure enough: 'Well, I do have this thing with the car radio – I have to have the volume set on on an even number like 8, or a number that's divisible by 5, like 10 or 15...' I tell him not to worry – (12) .... perfectly normal.

[1]Behaviour that is *hard-wired* is programmed, rather than learned.

164 Complete these newspaper stories with words from the box.

> had   had it not been   hardly   little   should   so   such

Fans over-eager to greet their hero

(1) .... had their hero's plane stopped moving when thousands of fans broke through police cordons and ran across the runway. A police spokesman admitted later that the incident could have ended in disaster. '(2) .... the fans invaded the runway a minute or two earlier, there might well have been a number of serious injuries.' (3) .... is the star's current popularity that many of the fans had waited all night at the airport.

Holiday chaos on the roads

A combination of warm weather and a public holiday has caused chaos on the country's motorways. (4) .... crowded is the main coast road, that police broadcast the following statement: '(5) .... you be thinking of setting off for the coast, we advise you to avoid the motorways at all costs and find alternative routes if at all possible.'

Family saved, thanks to 7-year-old's quick thumbs

A mother praised the technical skills of her seven-year-old son Tom, after the boy sent a text message telling the emergency services that the family car had been involved in an accident 100 kilometres from the nearest town. '(6) .... did we realise how useful it could be to be able to write a text message. (7) .... for Tom's quick thinking and quick thumbs, we probably wouldn't have survived the night.'

165 Look at the underlined sections in these short dialogues. Correct any errors. If the section is correct, write ✓.

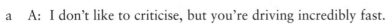

a A: I don't like to criticise, but you're driving incredibly fast.
   B: (1) <u>It may seem fast to you, but at no time since we left home I've broken the speed limit.</u>
   A: Oh no!
   B: What's the matter?
   A: (2) <u>There goes a police car.</u> He's right behind us. He wants us to stop!

b A: Why were you late for work?
   B: (3) <u>The first bus didn't come, and nor did the second one.</u>
   A: So what did you do?
   B: (4) <u>I kept waiting, then along three came at the same time.</u>

c A: Do you ever use the Internet to find things out?

   B: Sometimes, but if I'm in hurry to look something up, I ask my ten-year-old daughter.
      (5) <u>She's much quicker than am I at finding information.</u>

   A: That's not really surprising, is it?

   B: (6) <u>No, children are often better at these things than their parents are.</u>

d A: Oh no! (7) <u>There my lunch goes!</u>

   B: What do you mean?

   A: (8) <u>The dog's just eaten my sandwiches.</u>

e A: (9) <u>The phone goes there.</u> Shall I answer it?

   B: Thanks. That's very kind of you.

1 ....   6 ....
2 ....   7 ....
3 ....   8 ....
4 ....   9 ....
5 ....

166 **Complete the article with appropriate phrases from the box.**

| in walked | little do they | neither do | no sooner | not until | off he went |

(1) .... the technology lets us down do we realise how dependent on computers we have become. And when things do go wrong, what is the first thing we do? Panic of course, because, unless we are highly-trained computer scientists, we just don't know what to do. There must be a few individuals lucky enough to know computer experts personally, but I certainly don't and (2) .... any of my friends. The last time my computer crashed I got someone from a local firm to come and fix it for me. I'll never forget it. I opened the door and (3) .... a smart-looking young man dressed in a dark suit. Ten minutes later (4) .... again saying I'd have no more trouble with my computer. You can imagine what happened. (5) .... had I switched on the computer and logged on to the Internet than a familiar message appeared on the screen: 'Error of type 4457 has occurred. Contact technical support immediately.'

Of course there are still people around who don't have a computer or know how to use one. (6) .... know how lucky they are.

167 Rewrite the underlined sections of this email, starting with the words or phrases given, and using inversion where necessary.

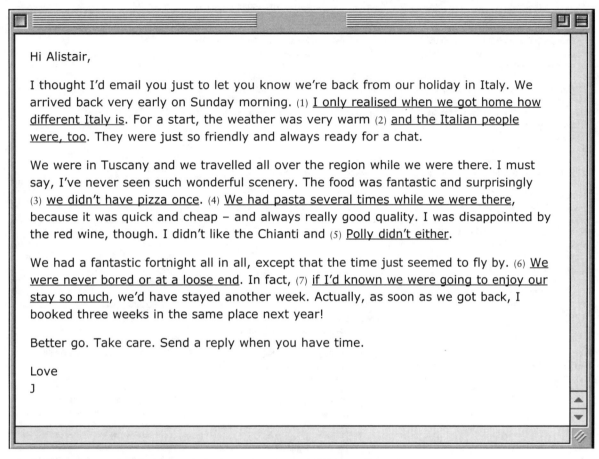

Hi Alistair,

I thought I'd email you just to let you know we're back from our holiday in Italy. We arrived back very early on Sunday morning. (1) I only realised when we got home how different Italy is. For a start, the weather was very warm (2) and the Italian people were, too. They were just so friendly and always ready for a chat.

We were in Tuscany and we travelled all over the region while we were there. I must say, I've never seen such wonderful scenery. The food was fantastic and surprisingly (3) we didn't have pizza once. (4) We had pasta several times while we were there, because it was quick and cheap – and always really good quality. I was disappointed by the red wine, though. I didn't like the Chianti and (5) Polly didn't either.

We had a fantastic fortnight all in all, except that the time just seemed to fly by. (6) We were never bored or at a loose end. In fact, (7) if I'd known we were going to enjoy our stay so much, we'd have stayed another week. Actually, as soon as we got back, I booked three weeks in the same place next year!

Better go. Take care. Send a reply when you have time.

Love
J

1 Only *when we got home did I realise how different Italy is.*
2 as ....
3 not ....
4 Several ....
5 neither ....
6 At no time ....
7 had ....

168 Write your own email to a friend telling them about something you did that you found interesting, exciting or just different. Use as many of these sentence beginnings as you can.

At no time,...	Nor did...
Neither...	Little did...
Only later / then,...	Not for one moment did...

Key

1

1 look / 're (are) looking
2 hear
3 're (are) doing
4 run / 'm (am) running
5 enjoy / 'm (am) enjoying (*I'm enjoying* suggests the speaker is happy with the experience so far, but this situation may or may not continue.)
6 don't regret / aren't regretting / 're not regretting (The present continuous would suggest a possible recent change of mind.)
7 (must) admit (The modal *must* can be used here to make the meaning more tentative.)
8 realise / 'm (am) realising (*I'm realising* suggests a recent growing awareness.)
9 just wonder / 'm (am) just wondering
10 're (are) looking
11 don't want
12 'm (am) thinking
13 want
14 confess / must confess (The modal *must* can be used here to make the meaning more tentative.)
15 'm (am) having / have
16 'm (am) considering
17 need
18 don't really want
19 believe
20 expect

2A

1 g 2 i 3 b 4 f 5 j 6 e
7 c 8 a 9 d 10 h

2B

1 always cost
2 I always feel
3 I'm expecting (= I'm going to have a baby)
4 Both answers are possible but *You're always taking* is more likely, as this use of the present continuous with *always* describes characteristic behaviour that the speaker finds annoying.
5 I feel / I'm feeling
6 is costing
7 We expect / We're expecting
8 I weigh
9 I always take
10 I'm weighing

3

1 This is an extract from a live commentary on a football match – a radio commentator is describing a penalty kick.
2 A TV reporter or a police spokesperson is commenting on video footage of a police raid.
3 This is a newspaper, radio or TV news headline.
4 This is a personal story told by the victim of a theft at a cash machine.
5 This is a joke.

4

Answer: The driver manages to avoid hitting the man because in fact it's daylight. The first part of the story leads us to believe it's dark.

1 is going (*goes* is also possible.)
2 is walking (*walks* is also possible.)
(In examples 1 and 2, the present continuous is more natural as the first two sentences set the scene, or provide the background, to what follows. However, the present simple can also be used if the speaker wishes to present these as the first two events in the story.)
3 isn't shining
4 is wearing
5 comes
6 doesn't have / does not have
7 sees
8 swerves
9 notices
10 continues

5

Example answers:

Picture 2 She's pleased with herself for being decisive and she says to herself: 'That's it. I can't change my mind now. It's irrevocable.'
Picture 3 She's walking back home, when she starts to worry. 'Am I doing the right thing?' she wonders.
Picture 4 'Paul's not a such a bad bloke,' she thinks. 'I don't really want to end the relationship.' Finally, she turns round and goes back to the postbox.
Picture 5 She waits for nearly two hours.
Picture 6 She's getting more and more anxious, when the postman finally arrives, gets out of the van and starts emptying the box. Loads of letters fall out. She tells him her story, asks for the letter back and says: 'It's a white envelope with blue writing.'

6

1 Have you had
2 I didn't sleep
3 I've checked
4 I took
5 I've never had
6 You revised
7 I've failed
8 I've ever taken
9 you've been waiting for
10 You've passed / You passed
(*You've passed* would be the most natural answer – showing the speaker's reaction to breaking news. *You passed* suggests that the speaker is simply passing on news of a past event.)
11 I really thought

7

2 lifted off
3 have been removed
4 instructed / have instructed
5 have agreed / have voted
6 reached / agreed

7 walked out
8 have voted (*have agreed* is also possible, but less natural than *have voted*.)
9 has admitted
10 pleaded / has pleaded
11 sent

8A

1 c 2 d 3 e 4 b 5 a

8B

1 I 2 E 3 I 4 P 5 I

9

Example answers:

1 ...there are some I can't bear to get rid of.
2 ...I was too embarrassed.
3 ...it's Friday already and I've heard nothing.

10

(Errors are underlined and numbered below. Corrections are given separately.)

a (no errors)
b No, (1) I'd looked out of the window at the time – wondering where we were
c Are you all right? You look as though (2) you've cried.
(3) My brother's been having a motorbike accident, and he's had to go to hospital.
d (4) We haven't been running out of coffee again, have we?
e (5) Have you played my guitar while I was out?
f (6) How many times had you been taking your driving test before you passed?
g (7) Yes, I've been belonging to this club since it opened 25 years ago.
h (8) He'd talked about me behind my back for the last two weeks or more.

Corrections:
(1) No, I'd been looking out / I was looking out
(2) you've been crying
(3) My brother's had a motorbike accident
(4) We haven't run out of coffee again
(5) Have you been playing
(6) had you taken / did you take
(7) I've belonged
(8) He'd been talking / He's been talking about me

11

(Where more than one answer is possible, the first answer given is the tense used in the original text. While the past simple is possible in many cases, using a wider range of tenses is preferred in good writing.)

1 began
2 was developing (*was developing* describes a situation which was changing or unfolding over a period of time. *developed* or *had developed* are also possible.)
3 turned out
4 was driving / drove
5 reopened
6 had been
7 was (Having diabetes is a permanent condition so the past perfect tense would be inappropriate here.)

8 had had (This returns the reader to the time in the past before Gary Barnicott arrived.) (*had* is also possible.)

9 had run out (This continues the sequence of events in the past before Gary Barnicott arrived.) (*ran out* is also possible.)

10 had lost (This continues the sequence of events in the past before Gary Barnicott arrived.) (*lost* is also possible.)

11 started

12 accompanied

13 checked

14 went

15 had broken down (This continues the sequence of events in the past before Gary Barnicott arrived.) (*broke down* is also possible.)

16 took

17 stopped

18 needed

19 had prepared (This is something Gary Barnicott did before going out that night.) (*prepared* is also possible.)

20 gave

21 had not eaten or drunk

22 lived (*were living* is also possible, though less likely, as it would imply that they were temporary residents.)

23 had come (This probably happened before Gary Barnicott arrived.) (*came* and *were coming* are also possible. *came* would suggest that the people came out while Barnicott was there. *were coming* would suggest that more and more people gradually came out.)

24 had been waiting (This emphasises that the waiting went on for a long time.) (*had waited* is also possible. This simply relates the fact that people waited.)

12

1 hadn't been / wasn't (The past perfect suggests that we are going to be told the background to this decision. The past perfect is often used at the beginning of narratives in this way. The past simple would be more common in a spoken narrative or in informal writing.)

2 had been thinking

3 was getting

4 I had started / I started (The past perfect indicates that the writer is going back to the beginning of his story. The past simple indicates a simple completed action in the past.)

5 really enjoyed

6 had worn off

7 broke

8 had

9 didn't miss

10 decided

11 had been

12 hurt / was hurting (*hurt* suggests a pain which came on quite suddenly. *was hurting* suggests a pain which gradually got worse.)

13 sat down

14 sat / was sitting

15 had only recently given up

16 had had to

17 decided

18 assured

19 did not regret / hadn't regretted (The past simple implies that there were no regrets at the time of speaking. The past perfect implies that there were no regrets at any point since making the decision.)

20 lived / was living

21 I had decided

22 had even finished

23 I'd been planning

13

Example answers:
In the end it was actually a very easy decision to make.
I'd been thinking about changing jobs ever since the time when my boss and I had a major disagreement about my responsibilities.
I'd been telling myself to look for something more worthwhile for some time.
The situation was becoming more and more intolerable.
I'd asked various people for their advice and they'd all told me to look for something better. What finally persuaded me was an email from my boss telling me that they were reducing my salary.

14

3 I was wondering / I've been wondering

4 has happened

5 's (has) told / told

6 ✓

7 was / had been

8 wants

9 He's been getting

10 ✓

11 moved

12 thinks

13 ✓

14 's (is) still trying

15 ✓

16 That sounds

17 hasn't even filled

15

1 've (have) been getting on

2 left

3 finished

4 found / was finding (*was finding* implies in the later stages.)

5 were

6 'd (had) just graduated

7 were

8 treated

9 've (have) been looking for

10 've (have) phoned up

11 've (have) replied / replied

12 found

13 comes

14 've (have) begun

15 's (is) sending / 's (has) been sending / sends

16 works / 's (is) working / 's (has) worked / 's (has) been working

17 have

18 needs

19 'd (had) been using / used / was using

20 's (has) all started

16

1 was working / worked

2 'd (had) worked / 'd (had) been working

3 became

4 was starting / started

5 'd (had) never been / was never

6 complained

7 agreed

8 warned

9 'd (had) not returned

10 phoned

11 had said / said

12 'd (had) actually turned up

13 came / had come

14 used / had used / had been using / was using

15 uses

16 have been escaping / are escaping / have escaped

17 are cooking / have been cooking / have cooked (*have been cooking* suggests over a period of time, whereas *have cooked* suggests that the chef's insides are completely cooked and is therefore less suitable.)

17

Example answer:
38-year-old man escapes fire

18

Example stories:

1 More than fifty families have been trapped in their homes since their village was hit by floods at the weekend. The rain started on Friday evening and did not stop until early Monday morning. The stream which runs through the village burst its banks on Sunday night and water has been rushing uncontrollably through the streets ever since. Most of the trapped families have now moved to upstairs rooms and are waiting for the floods to subside before starting the clear-up operation.

2 Millions of business computers across the world have been attacked by a virus which is threatening to bring international trade to a standstill. The first companies to be affected were in Australia, suggesting that its creator may either live in that region or have a grudge against a particular Australian business. Since then, the virus has appeared in places as far apart as Buenos Aires in Argentina and Helsinki in Finland. It is thought that the virus travels by email and is programmed to empty the hard drive of its victim's computers.

19

Example answer:
Bank robber arrested
A man in his late forties was arrested late yesterday afternoon as he attempted to dispose of money he had stolen earlier in the day. Police officers arrested the man as he was about to throw a bag of bank notes from a bridge to a boat on the river below, where an accomplice was waiting.

On Tuesday morning the man had walked calmly into a town centre bank holding a revolver and threatening to shoot staff and customers unless he was given one million pounds in cash.

Fortunately, all the money was recovered and nobody was injured.

20

1 d   2 e   3 b   4 f   5 g
6 a   7 c

21

2 Yes, but what if I've done really badly and fail / I fail?

3 Their new car's (has) got / Their new car has / Their new car's (is) going to have / Their new car will have seven seats.

4 I expect she'll (will) have been thinking about her job.

5 The concert starts at 7.30.

6 Suppose you never see her again?

7 Levels (of ozone) will continue to rise for another 10 to 15 years, unless drastic action is taken immediately.

8 Are you going / Will you go / Will you be going to France this summer as usual?

9 Will you come again soon?

10 He'll be wondering why he bothered.

11 She'll be wishing she stayed / had stayed at home.

22

2 're (are) you going to do / 're (are) you doing

3 'm (am) going to meet / 'm (am) meeting

4 we'll get

5 'll (will) need / 'll (will) be needing

6 'll (will) go / 'm (am) going

7 'll (will) be / 's (is) going to be (*will* suggests this is the speaker's opinion. *be going to* suggests a prediction based on evidence, such as seeing a weather forecast.)

8 'll (will) end up / end up

9 are you going to do / are you doing

10 won't have

11 'll (will) give

12 'm (am) going to finish

13 won't want

14 'll (will) be

23

(Errors are underlined and numbered below. Corrections are given separately.)

(1) <u>We're going to leave</u> tomorrow so we thought we'd let you all know (2) <u>where we're going to go</u>, and how you can contact us.
(3) <u>We're picking up emails</u> from time to time if we can find an internet café, and our address is, as usual: samncharlie@worldoutthere.com. We'll take the new mobile, which is 04453 565423, in case (4) <u>you will need</u> to get hold of us.

(5) <u>We will have taken off</u> from London early tomorrow morning and fly to Delhi. By Sunday evening (6) <u>we'll watch</u> an Indian sunset over the Taj Mahal! We'll be in India for two weeks, and are planning to visit

Jaipur, Goa, Bombay and Darjeeling if we have time.

Then we go to Singapore, arriving there on 15th April, and we're going to spend a couple of days there before flying on to Sydney. (7) <u>We'll travel</u> 13,000 miles by then, and we'll be exploring Down Under for a full three weeks. Then it's a long flight across the Pacific, and we'll arrive in San Francisco on 10th May. (Sal, (8) <u>we won't have been forgetting</u> your birthday on the 9th, promise, but forgive us if we send something from Australia and (9) <u>it will arrive</u> late!)

We're spending a month criss-crossing North America by car and plane, but finally on 12th June (10) <u>we'll have left</u> JFK in New York on our final flight home.

(11) <u>We're calling</u> each of you from time to time. Keep in touch, and we'll be thinking of you all while we're away.

Corrections:

(1) We're leaving
(2) (Though *where we're going to go* is possible, *where we're going* would be the more usual form.)
(3) We'll be picking up emails / We'll pick up emails
(4) in case you need
(5) We're taking off / We'll take off / We'll be taking off / We take off
(6) we'll be watching
(7) We'll have travelled
(8) we won't forget
(9) it arrives late
(10) we'll leave / we'll be leaving / we leave
(11) We'll call / We'll be calling

24

Example answers:
I leave / I'm leaving here at five in the morning.
This time tomorrow I'll be in Tokyo.
In a week's time I'll be on top of the Empire State Building!
On 1st May I'll be dancing in the streets of Rio.
Once in a while I'm going to treat myself to a luxury hotel.
When I get to Tokyo, I'm going to try a sushi bar.

25A

1 d   2 c   3 g   4 b   5 f
6 a   7 e

25B

a not acceptable (Weather cannot be controlled by humans so *be to* is not appropriate.)

b acceptable

c acceptable

d acceptable

e not acceptable (A continuous form is less likely to express something you want to do.)

f not acceptable (*Shall* is possible, but less common in this fairly informal context.)

g acceptable

26

2 the champion is set to take her place

3 the Chelsea manager is on the brink of leaving the club

4 but he was to play in 22 more

5 James Grayson intends / is intending to leave

6 is to close

7 is looking to transfer

8 she aims to be

9 has guaranteed (spectators) that he will refund / has guaranteed to refund

10 we shall get it back!

27A

Suggested answers:

2 a F
Name cards <u>are to be arranged</u> in alphabetical order.
2 b I
Please <u>arrange</u> name cards in alphabetical order.
3 a I
<u>You know</u> that you <u>shouldn't carry</u> knives, scissors or other sharp objects onto the aircraft, <u>don't you</u>?
3 b F
<u>Passengers shall not</u> carry knives, scissors or other sharp objects <u>on board the aircraft</u>.

27B

Suggested answers:

1 a I
We <u>were supposed to</u> get to the hotel by seven, but the snow <u>got worse and worse</u> and <u>we got later and later</u>.
1 b L
We <u>were to have arrived</u> at the house by seven, but as the snow <u>grew heavier</u>, the journey became longer and longer.
2 a L
I am <u>determined that she shall see you</u>, no matter what her doctor has decided.
2 b I
<u>She'll</u> see you, <u>whatever</u> her doctor says.
3 a I
She <u>was supposed to</u> give him the ring, but the more she saw him, the less she liked him and in the end <u>she didn't</u>!
3 b L
She <u>was to have given him</u> the ring, but her <u>dislike of him</u> grew and she did not.

28

1 's (is) due to arrive / 's (is) bound to arrive / 's (is) sure to arrive. (*due to* suggests that it is now the time she was scheduled to arrive, while *bound to* and *sure to* indicate certainty that she will arrive soon.)

2 was on the point of filling in

3 's (is) sure to get / 's (is) bound to get / 'll (will) get (*will* indicates a prediction, while *sure to* and *bound to* suggest greater certainty.)

4 be on the point of doing / be on the brink of doing (*on the brink of* is often used when someone is about to do something important or extraordinary.)

5 's (is) bound to want / 's (is) sure to want / 'll (will) want / 'll (will) be wanting

29
Your own ideas. See model text.

30
2 'm (am) allowed to / 'm (am) able to
3 could / might
4 can't / couldn't.
5 can / am able to / am allowed to (All forms are possible, but *can* is more likely in an informal context such as an email. *am able to* in this context means *am allowed to* by the authorities.)
6 can / are able to (Both forms are possible, but *can* is more likely in an informal context such as an email.)
7 can / am able to (Both forms are possible, but *can* is more likely in an informal context such as an email.)
8 can't (*could* is also possible, with the implied meaning: *I could tell you about everything I've seen and done, but there just isn't time.*)
9 couldn't / wasn't able to / wasn't allowed to (*wasn't able to* in this context means *wasn't allowed to* by the authorities.)
10 can / could / am able to / am allowed to
11 can / could / will be able to / will be allowed to
12 can / could
13 can / are able to (Both forms are possible, but *are able to* is rather formal for this context.)

31
2 What would have happened
3 ✓
4 I just couldn't manage it. (*I just wasn't able to manage it* is possible, but *I just couldn't manage it* is more likely in speech.
5 I could hear
6 ✓
7 I was able to go out
8 The painkillers will have helped
9 Maggie will be at home
10 ✓

32
1 will
2 might / would (*would* implies that the speaker is certain about this. *might* suggests that the speaker thinks there is a possibility of this.)
3 would / used to
4 will
5 may / might
6 might / may / will (*will* implies that the speaker is certain about this. *may / might* suggests that the speaker thinks there is a possibility of this.)
7 will
8 would / used to
9 would / used to
10 Ø
11 won't
12 will / might / may (*will* implies that the speaker is certain about this. *may / might* suggests that the speaker thinks there is a possibility of this.)
13 wouldn't

33
Your own answers. See example.

(Note: Both the present simple and *will* can both be used to talk about characteristic behaviour. *used to* is used with states (*be bossy*) and *would* is used with repeated actions.)

34
1 can't
2 could have
3 couldn't
4 won't
5 will
6 would
7 won't
8 will
9 used to be
10 may / might
11 Are you likely to see
12 Could

35
1 = You should expect boys to behave like typical boys.
2 = It's impossible to keep a secret or lie for very long.
3 = There's no sure way of preventing accidents.
4 = People whose ambition it is to become police officers.
5 The speaker is suggesting that he/she doesn't believe the excuse for doing poorly in the exam.

36
1 a (a possibility – one of our ideas)
2 b (a suggestion)
3 b (a complaint after the event)
4 a (an uncertainty)
5 b (some compensation for the fact that the weather wasn't good)
6 a (a deduction about the weather based on evidence)
7 a (uncertainty about a present situation)
8 b (future possibility)

37
1 can
2 being able to
3 can (= be able to) / may (= it's possible)
4 will
5 may
6 may / might
7 may
8 used to (This is referring to a past state that has changed so *would* is not correct here.)
9 could / might
10 may
11 might
12 can
13 could
14 can / may
15 will
16 may / could

38
Example answers:
1 I can use spreadsheets because I've had to learn them for my job. (In this sentence *can* is used to talk about ability.)
I can vote because I am now over 18. (In this sentence *can* is used to talk about permission.)
2 I could touch my toes while keeping my legs straight when I was a child, but it's impossible now. (In this sentence *could* is used to talk about ability.)
I could travel on buses for nothing, and get into museums without paying when I was a child. (In this sentence *could* refers to permission.)
3 I'd love to be able to fly a plane, but getting a pilot's licence is an expensive business!

39
2 must we endure
3 Ought we to put up with
4 Should we stand back
5 must be spending
6 I need hardly remind you
7 should have had
8 Ought I to stand back
9 Need I go on?

40
Your own answers. See example.
(Note the use of *they* to mean 'people in the government'.)

41
1 must have been getting
2 should've
3 should
4 you've got to go
5 don't need to
6 (Both are possible. *has to be taken out* is slightly less formal.)
7 wouldn't
8 (Both are possible.)
9 needn't (*need hardly to* is correct but too formal for this context.)
10 (Both are possible. *You've got to make sure* sounds more insistent.)
11 should I (*need I* is correct but too formal for this context. *Who do I need to contact* would be more natural.)
12 must

42
1 have to play
2 had to go out / needed to go out / must have gone out / must have had to go out
3 do you have to / do you need to / have you got to (less formal)
4 needn't cost much / doesn't have to cost much
5 must be / has to be
6 must be having
7 'd (had) better go out
8 must be

123

43

Example answers:

2 You needn't bother. I'm driving 200km tomorrow and it will only get dirty again.
3 You needn't / don't need to do that – you can use mine.
4 You didn't need to wear a suit. The invitation said 'informal dress'.
5 You don't need to / needn't be afraid. I've done this dive loads of times.
6 You needn't have worried. She hardly ever uses it any more.
7 No. I didn't need to get anything so I came straight home.

44

1 look / seem
2 went
3 doesn't seem / doesn't appear
4 's (is) getting
5 's (has) got / 's (is) getting
6 isn't getting / 's (is) not getting
7 kept
8 sounds / seems / is
9 went
10 seems / appears

45

1 become
2 gone
3 to be burying
4 seems to be / seems
5 looks
6 turned
7 gone
8 got
9 became
10 sound
11 look / appear
12 turned out (*turn out + to be; end up + being*)
13 stay
14 keep
15 becoming / getting (*getting* is more informal.)
16 becoming / getting (*getting* is more informal.)

46

Example answers:

1 ...to have become more serious.
...to have better jobs than me.
2 ...to be interested in politics.
...to be doing anything to keep fit.
3 ...more interested in the environment.
...less obsessed with making money.
4 ...a more pleasant place to live.
...busier and noisier.
5 ...that there's no place like home.
...that friends are very important to me.

47A

2 c 3 a 4 f 5 e 6 j 7 d
8 h 9 g 10 b

47B

Example answers:

2 It isn't important, or isn't known, *who* encourages people.
3 The passive allows us to omit the use of people as a subject.
4 The subject (*Being able to call...*) is already known, and using the passive avoids repeating it.
5 The passive lets us put a long subject (*how quickly the idea was adopted*) at the end of the sentence.

48

1 are being disturbed
2 is believed
3 has been described / is described / is being described
4 suffered (*Suffer* does not have a passive form.)
5 was taken
6 jumped
7 bit
8 described being chased / described having been chased
9 was seen
10 is living
11 are thought to be / are thought to have been
12 has not yet been established
13 are tamed

49

Example answer:

In December, we were voted the best educational establishment in the area, and rated by the Department of Education as one of the top twenty-five colleges in the country. In March, the college was offered the services of two top managers from a local company. Students on the Advanced Business Studies course will be taught by them in the run-up to the summer exams.
In May, we were mentioned by the Minster of Education as an example of excellence, and our teaching methods and exam results were described as outstanding. Also in May, we were asked by our twin college in France to send a group of ten students to their exam ceremony. In late June, Hilary Edwards was appointed principal from next September.
In July, we were invited to send five students to the International Students Congress in New York, rounding off a truly memorable year for the college.

50A

A2 B4 C1 D3

50B

(Note: In these news reports it is common for the story to start with the present perfect to introduce events, and then use the past simple to give the details.)

A
1 it has been confirmed
2 it was also revealed
3 it was stressed

4 reflected / reflects
5 it was reported
6 were said / are said
7 refused

B
1 has destroyed
2 is thought
3 have been started
4 were soaked / had been soaked
5 extinguished
6 were called back
7 were re-ignited (passive: if an unknown person started it again deliberately) / re-ignited (active: if the fire started again by itself)

C
1 have emerged
2 was found
3 were treated
4 punished
5 be reinspected
6 has been threatened
7 are seen

D
1 has been reported
2 was seen
3 (was) observed
4 arrived
5 It is estimated / It has been estimated
6 it is believed
7 has been targeted

51

1 g What is your idea of perfect happiness?
2 k Which living person do you most admire? (Or less commonly: *What living person do you most admire?*)
3 h And who do you despise?
4 e How often does your group play these days?
5 c Where do you enjoy playing most?
6 f How about large concert halls?
7 d When did you start playing?
8 i How many different bands have you played in?
9 b Why did you decide to bring out a solo CD after so long?
10 j How surprised were you to be nominated for this fantastic award?
11 a Who has bought the CD?
12 l how would you like to be remembered?

52

2 You're going where?
3 Would it be a good idea to get a taxi? / Wouldn't it be a good idea to get a taxi? / Would it not be a good idea to get a taxi?
4 You've done what? / You did what?
5 Why do you never save (any of your pocket money)?
6 They get how much?
7 why don't you get (yourself) a part-time job? / why not get (yourself) a part-time job?
8 Why don't you look in the newspaper? / Why not look in the newspaper?
9 You're (too) what?

53

Suggested answers:

1 Hasn't the weather been terrible / turned nasty!
2 Why didn't you tell me you'd had an accident in the car? / Why didn't you tell me about the accident in the car?
3 Whose is that/this MP3 player? / Whose MP3 player is this/that? / Who does this/that MP3 player belong to?
4 How was the interview? / How did the interview go? / How do you feel / think the interview went? / What was the interview like?
5 Who (do you think) is ringing (us) at this time of night? / Who could it be ringing (us) at this time of night?
6 Didn't we have a fantastic time (at the zoo)!
7 What if we miss our flight? / What shall we do if we miss our flight? / What happens if we miss our flight?
8 Who were you talking to on the phone when I came in? (*To whom were you talking when I came in?* is also possible but less likely because it is very formal.)
9 Whose car was the bomb discovered under?
10 Which (one) of the contestants won the competition?

54

2 mistaken her
3 believed her (to be)
4 based ... on
5 considered her
6 detract from
7 culminated in
8 declared himself
9 refused (her)
10 permitted (her)
11 reminding ... of
12 pronounced the trial / hearing
13 judged the verdict
14 inflicted ... on

55

2 We have varied our product ranges.
3 (*Fall* cannot be used transitively when it means decrease. An alternative might be: *We have lowered our costs, and (have) decreased our prices.*)
4 (*Newspapers and magazines have moved to the front of our stores* might be found in colloquial English but could imply that they moved by themselves! An alternative is the passive: *Newspapers and magazines have been moved to the front of our stores.*)
5 (*Create* cannot be used intransitively. An alternative is the passive: *New products have been created.*)

56

2 differentiate between / deal with
3 base ... on
4 point out to
5 belonged to
6 regard .... as

7 dealing with
8 explain to
9 aspired to
10 culminate in

57

1 ask the children for their homework
2 (Both are possible.)
3 make models with clay for the children
4 Demonstrate this to them
5 (Both are possible.)
6 ask them to sing
7 (Both are possible.)
8 Describe the characters to them
9 Choose a suitable book for each child
10 Leave the lesson record for me. (*leave something to someone = give something to someone after you die*)

58

2 to impersonate / to stand in for
3 of passing
4 to get away with
5 to be
6 to impersonating / to standing in for
7 taking (*taking* would be more likely than *take* since the inspector would be unlikely to watch the whole of each test.)
8 (to) obtaining / (to) having obtained
9 (from) doing / (from) getting away with

59

2 Harris denied taking / having taken the driving tests.
3 Anna had tried to discourage him from doing it / from taking the tests.
4 Harris refused to own up to / didn't own up to / wouldn't own up to what he had done
5 Harris persuaded / had persuaded Dave to let him take the test for him.
6 Dave didn't object / hadn't objected (to Harris taking the test for him).
7 Dave admitted wanting to pass (the test) at any cost.
8 The judge accused Harris of endangering / having endangered the lives of thousands of motorists.
9 The judge sentenced Harris to six months in prison in order to deter others from doing the same thing / from copying his actions.
10 The judge hoped that the sentence would prevent anything like this from (ever) happening again.

60

2 I knew (that) they would disapprove of me / my working abroad.
3 They have always let me make my own decisions.
4 I even considered not turning up for the interview.
5 The American company had arranged for the interviews to be held / had arranged to hold the interviews in London.
6 In the end I decided not to work in the USA. / In the end it was me who decided not to work in the USA.

61

1 trying
2 hitting (This suggests that there was repeated hitting.) / hit (This suggests that the person hit the steering wheel once only.)
3 shouting (This suggests that there was repeated shouting.) / shout (This suggests that the person shouted once only.)
4 striking (This suggests that the person struck the steering wheel repeatedly.) / strike (This suggests that the person struck the steering wheel once only.)
5 punching (continuously)
6 shouting (This suggests that there was repeated shouting.)
(*shout* is not possible because in the following sentence Ms Prochak refers back to this, saying: *No, but I knew he was (shouting).*)
7 opening and closing
8 get out
9 slam
10 walk
11 pouring (This suggests that the woman saw part of the action only.)
pour (This suggests that the woman saw the entire action from beginning to end.)
12 explode

62

Example answers:

2 On the train the other day, I overheard a couple talking about emigrating to Siberia.
3 While we were driving along the motorway recently, we saw a lorry burst into flames.
4 On our visit to the wildlife park, we watched chimpanzees playing in a tree.
5 As I walked through the crowds of people, I felt someone put their hand in my pocket to take my wallet.

63

2 they promised (that) they wouldn't make / they promised not to make
3 whether my partner was listening / would be listening
4 asked (me) what the capital of Nepal was called
5 asked (me) if / whether I knew two countries where you can / could find
6 wanted to know the winner
7 asked (me) why Muhammad Ali didn't box / hadn't boxed
8 asked (me) if / whether the sun was
9 wondered if / whether I could name

64

Suggested answers:

2 He believed (that) having real sets was really important / (that) it was important to have real sets.
3 He admitted (that) they had lots of problems / we've got lots of problems (*we've got* suggests mankind as a whole.)
4 He agreed (that) it was very important to have the co-operation of the Dahl family.
5 He disagreed (that) Johnny's Willy Wonka bore / bears a resemblance to Michael Jackson.

6 He explained (to the interviewer) that the more modern approach would probably be / would probably have been to do the Oompa-Loompas with computer animation.
7 He added that this seemed to fit with the Roald Dahl universe.
8 The interviewer suggested (to Burton) (that) his films had become less dark.

65

2 to them (or both items left blank)
3 me
4 what
5 me (that)
6 that (or leave blank)
7 myself (that)
8 what
9 what
10 me
11 that

66

(For information on quoting, see Appendix 3 in *Advanced Grammar in Use*.)
Ella came back into the room.
"Have you seen him?" Alex asked, and she nodded.
"He was in the garden," she replied, "so I went up and told him."
"What exactly did you say?" asked Alex.
"I said I wasn't going to Sweden with him - I thought it was better to be direct," replied Ella.
Alex looked impatient, and asked, "But how did he react?"
"Not very well, of course," said Ella, and she smiled knowingly.

67

Example answers:
1 Sue checked whether Philip had been at home, and told him about new coffee stains on the carpet upstairs. Philip denied that he'd been upstairs.
2 The manager informed the employees that the company was closing the factory, and they assumed they would be losing their jobs, but he reassured them that they would be relocated to other larger factories.
3 Sarah confided that she thought he'd made the wrong decision, and Jo agreed, but Sarah warned her he would be furious if she told him.
4 The manager requires / required them to be at work by 7.00, and expects / expected them to stay until 15.30.
5 The man pointed out that his neighbour's car was blocking his / The man pointed out to his neighbour that her car was blocking his, but the neighbour confessed she'd locked her key inside, and the man suggested calling / suggested (to her) (that) they call the breakdown services.
6 The defendant, Jack, complained that he hadn't been treated fairly, and his friend said s/he understood the evidence to be incomplete, but the judge considered the case (to be) closed.

68

1 a, b   2 b   3 b, c   4 a, c
5 a   6 b   7 a   8 b, c   9 a, b, c

69

1 sure / sure that / sure whether / certain / certain that / certain whether
2 adamant that (*adamant* suggests strong feeling and certainty, but adjectives such as *sure (that)* and *certain (that)* are also possible here.)
3 sympathetic to / towards
4 complimentary about
5 dismissive of / critical of
6 dismissive of / critical of
7 sure what / certain what
8 abusive about / critical of

70

1 Mike urged Jill to come out with everyone that night. He swore that everyone wanted to see her, and insisted that she came.
2 It was Marta's birthday, and Pete announced that he was going to surprise her at home. He volunteered to get flowers and chocolate for her, and (he) invited me to meet 20 minutes later outside her house.
3 Teresa longs to live in a warmer climate because she doesn't want to wear jumpers and coats all the time. She hopes she'll get the chance / She hopes to get the chance soon, and has revealed that her company is thinking of opening a branch in Greece.
4 Bob suggested that I (should) read something by JK Rowling, and offered to lend me her first novel. He recommended reading the whole series if I enjoyed that one.

71A

I shall / I'll fall asleep if this goes on much longer!

71B

1 He wondered whether they could bring the session to an end because he was starving.
2 She wrote (that) they mustn't let the others know what they were planning.
3 She admitted (that) she couldn't hear / hadn't been able to hear anything he had said.
4 She doubted whether / that they would be able to agree.
5 He was uncertain why they kept disagreeing.

72

1 (should) agree / promise / undertake
2 advisable / important / imperative / essential
3 (should) be
4 imperative / essential / important
5 (should) not blame
6 advisable
7 (should) be used
8 (should) choose / use
9 refer
10 conceivable

73A

Your own ideas.

73B

Your own answers. See example.

73C

Your own answers. See examples.

74

Example answers:
1 ...he should look after himself better. (This is an informal conversation, maybe between friends or neighbours, so it would be better to keep *should* in this context.)
2 ... (should) take a 5% reduction in pay.
3 ...(should) be taken on by the company (Items 2 and 3: This is a formal conversation between, for example, two company directors and an accountant. Omitting *should* would be quite natural in this context.)
4 ...I (should) receive a full refund. (This is a formal conversation between a dissatisfied customer and a shop assistant. Omitting *should* would be quite natural in this context.)
5 ...he should phone the police immediately. (This is an informal conversation, maybe between friends or neighbours, so it would be better to keep *should* in this context.)
6 serve (This is a very formal courtroom conversation between a judge and a convicted criminal. *Should* is better omitted here.)
7 ...that all children (should) be late no more than twice in any one week. (This is a conversation between a school attendance officer and a pupil's mother. The official's language is quite formal, whereas the mother's is quite informal. *Should* could be included or omitted in this context.)

75

2 has / have
3 wears / wear
4 win / wins
5 opens
6 is
7 builds / build

76

2 ✗ / Has
3 ✓ + has
4 ✓
5 ✗ / is
6 ✗ / say
7 ✗ / are (The noun *staff* usually takes a plural verb.)
8 ✗ / is
9 ✗ / was
10 ✓
11 ✓ + are finding
12 ✗ / has
13 ✓ + lives; ✓ + was
(In British English *couple* is usually followed by a plural verb, though in American English a singular is more commonly used. The choice of singular or plural should be consistent throughout a piece of writing.)

14 ✓
15 ✓ + is
16 ✓ + There are (In informal spoken English *There's* + plural noun is common.)
17 ✗ / aren't (*Police* referring to police officers in general is always plural. An alternative which usually takes a singular verb is the *police force*.)

77

Example answers:
1 A lot of people I know have taken up yoga.
2 The outskirts of the town where I live are full of expensive houses.
3 I think statistics are often used to support ridiculous ideas. / I think statistics is a very useful subject to study.
4 Banning smoking in public places is a very controversial issue.
5 I'm one of those people who worries / worry about anything and everything.
6 What worries me most about the future is the threat posed by global warming.

78

1 The singular verb is used because *Snow Drops* is a product brand name.
2 *Delta* is the name of a company. A plural verb has been chosen because companies can be thought of as groups of individual people.
3 *Essex Libraries* is the collective name for an organisation. *have* would also be possible here, but would mean individual branches of the library in different places.
4 *Windows* is the name of a famous computer system.
5 *half* represents a group of people.

79

2 The band + was formed + c (in the late nineties by Philippe Cohen-Solal.) / The band + creates + b (their unusual sound by combining dub and hip-hop influences with the sounds of talented Argentinian tango musicians).
3 XL Recordings, their record company, + is / are + a (a well-respected dance music label).
4 This unique trio, based in Paris + creates / create + b (their unusual sound by combining dub and hip-hop influences with the sounds of talented Argentinian tango musicians). / This unique trio, based in Paris, + were formed + c (in the late nineties by Philippe Cohen-Solal).
5 The music press worldwide + has given / have given / gives / give + g (their live performances ecstatic reviews).
6 A typical Gotan audience + consists + d (of people of all ages).
7 The majority of the people at their concerts just + listen + h (to the music, clapping along or swaying in their seats).
8 A few young people get up and move about, but usually it's the older generation who + dance + e (the tango in the aisles or at the front of the concert hall).

80

1 The editorial column of a serious newspaper; a letter to a newspaper.
2 The subject matter and choice of vocabulary make it obvious that this text is written in formal language. In addition, all the singular subjects have singular verbs and plural subjects have plural verbs. This is a feature of very correct language, regarded by some people as being pedantic or old-fashioned.
3 In less formal or less correct writing, the following might be used:
what is required to deal with this situation is new laws
A government sub-committee are currently working
Each of the committee members have

81

2 bookshop
3 town centre
4 chicken breasts
5 tin of tuna
6 tomato purée
7 two cupfuls / cupsful (*Cupfuls* is more usual in British English. Both *cupsful* or *cupfuls* are possible in American English.)
8 shopping list
9 teabags
10 tea leaves
11 glasses case
12 kitchen table
13 children's bedroom

82

In general, a phrase rather than a compound noun can be used if the compound noun is not generally known or used. This is sometimes the case with subject-related terminology. For example, the medical profession might use *blood flow and muscle temperature*, but the general public might prefer *the flow of blood* and *the temperature of muscles*.

A This text offers advice to people doing exercise. It is authoritatively scientific, but still comprehensible to someone with no scientific training.
1 Warm-up exercises
2 blood pressure
3 the flow of blood / the blood flow
4 muscle temperature / the temperature of muscles
5 a five-minute warm-up (*A warm-up of five minutes* is also possible, but not as natural.)
6 walking pace

B This is part of the introduction to a beginner's guide to the Internet. It is written in deliberately user-friendly language.
7 collection of computers (*Computer network* has been avoided because the writer considers it to be jargon.)
8 *24-hour connections* (This phrase is self-explanatory. *Connections open for 24 hours a day* sounds clumsy.)
9 *home computers* (Commonly used term which is likely to be familiar to all readers.)

C and D These are newspaper headlines, where compound forms rather than longer phrases are used to save space and to convey immediacy.
10 financial fraud cover-up
11 free school computer handout scheme

83

1 bicycle wheel
2 boys' school
3 ✓
4 parents-in-law / parent-in-laws
5 exercise machine
6 sit-ups and push-ups
7 kitchen floor

84

Example answers:
2 My favourite rooms are my *bedroom* and the *bathroom*.
3 In the kitchen, there's *a washing machine*, *a dishwasher*, *a food mixer* and a *coffee maker*.
4 The most comfortable places are the *armchair* in the *living room* and the *floor cushion* in my bedroom.
5 From my front door I can see *the main road*, *a bus stop*, *a car park* and the *post office*.

85

1 friend of mine
2 Managing Director
3 Sales Executive
4 summer we spent in Denmark
5 holiday I'll never forget
6 summer of 2001
7 horizon
(Note: This is the most likely order for items 4–6. *It's a holiday I'll never forget* refers back to the holiday in Denmark. In item 6 the speaker is merely checking the date.)
8 new car
9 Toyota
10 of those
11 past
12 Japanese cars
13 sun
14 Sunday morning (This suggests it's a typical activity on any Sunday. *Sunday morning* (zero article) can also be used to suggest this.)
15 hostas
16 mixture
17 sun and shade (*Sun* with no article = sunshine.)
18 first Monday after my birthday
19 morning
20 future

86

2 a / the
3 Ø
4 a
5 Ø
6 a / Ø
7 a
8 Ø (Use no article with *other* + plural noun)

9 Ø
10 a
11 the
12 the
13 a
14 the
15 a
16 Ø (We use zero article to talk generally about email, but note that we use *a/an* or *the* to refer to a specific email: *I got an email from Simon. I replied to the email straight away.*)
17 Ø
18 the
19 Ø
20 a

87

1 Ø / the (*The* emphasises that we are talking about the most famous person with that name.)
2 One
3 the
4 the
5 a
6 a
7 An
8 Ø
9 the
10 an
11 a / one
12 a
13 an
14 Ø
15 Ø
16 one
17 one
18 the
19 a (= a person called Graham Potter)
20 the
21 a (if the abbreviation is pronounced as a word) / an (if the abbreviation is spelt out letter by letter)
22 A
23 an
24 the

88A

1 this boy (*This* is used when characters are first introduced.)
2 This other boy (*This* is used when characters are first introduced.)
3 The first boy
4 the second boy

88B

Your own ideas. Use text in exercise 88A as a model.

89

Example answers:
2 no answer came
3 No amount of calling or searching ever revealed the fate of the passengers of the *Agnes Rose.*
4 much debate will focus / will be focussing
5 Many commentators

6 many a departing leader knows / many departing leaders know
7 Little is known
8 Few (humans) have ever seen them / Few have ever been seen (by humans)
9 fishermen take little notice

90

2 ✓ modern paintings all look the same
✓ all modern paintings look the same
✗ all of the modern paintings look the same
3 ✗ I've had few time
✓ I haven't had much time
✓ I've had little time. (This is less likely in this informal context.)
4 ✗ any luck
✓ no luck
5 ✓ there were none
✗ not any were
✓ there weren't any
6 ✓ was no answer (commonly used in this context)
✗ weren't any answer
✓ wasn't any answer
7 ✓ the whole week
✓ all week
✗ all the week
8 ✗ fewer than
✓ less than
9 ✓ a large number of
✓ many (This is grammatically correct but unlikely in informal spoken English.)
✓ lots of (This is the most likely, as this is informal spoken English.)
10 ✗ not any (We don't usually use not a / any after and.)
✓ no

91

1 no
2 nothing
3 entire
4 none
5 every
6 many
7 No

92

2 I wanted to make sure I had as good a chance + as anyone + a (to get some bargains).
3 There were lots of different things I was looking for, but + not all of them + f (were in the sale).
4 I was really pleased with everything I managed to get, especially considering + what little time + e (I had).
5 A friend said the sale was so popular that + no fewer than + d (5000 people came through the doors on that morning alone).
6 I spent + far too much + c and hope I won't regret it.

93

1 many
2 not
3 Every
4 every
5 every

6 many
7 many
8 any
9 every

94A

2 some
3 Little
4 each
5 A substantial amount of time / Plenty of time
6 A great deal of that
7 just over
8 not much time
9 less than

94B

Example answer:
The average trip to the shopping centre lasts some 3¹/4 hours. A considerable amount of time, over two hours, is spent in clothes and other shops. Less time, just half an hour, is devoted to eating and drinking in one of the cafés in the centre, and little time is spent just sitting down – just 7 minutes on average. Not much time is spent talking to friends that people meet, just 8 minutes, compared with the 15 minutes that each shopper spends talking on a mobile phone. Thankfully, hardly any time is spent paying for parking – just 3 minutes for the typical visitor.

95

1 *which* was published
2 *whose* quiet formality
3 people, *none of whom*
4 the skill *with which*
5 ✓
6 someone *who* possesses

96

1 *Midnight Strikes* is the perfect crime novel for anyone whose hero is Sherlock Holmes.
2 ... that the rather literary style which the book is written in will make it hard-going for those used to fast-moving blockbusters.
3 I suspect, in fact, that the readers (that) this book will most appeal to will probably be over the age of 30.
4 The story is set in the early part of the twentieth century, when the general population were quite unaware...
5 The villain of the novel devises a plan by which he gains / a plan which enables him to gain the trust of vulnerable people (that) he meets at church.
6 The character (that) many male readers will most closely identify with is Inspector Blakeman,...
7 The ending, which I can say nothing about, will come as a genuine surprise.

97

1 that
2 whatever
3 that
4 wherever
5 whenever / when
6 whichever

98A

1 which
2 where
3 which / that
4 when
5 who / that
6 which
7 which / that
8 which / that
9 who
10 who
11 which / that
12 which / that
13 who
14 which
15 which

98B

Only in item 11 could the relative pronoun be omitted. This is because it is the only relative pronoun which is the object (rather than the subject) of the relative clause.

99

(Additional information in italics.)
Ry Cooder, *who was born on March 15th, 1947 in Los Angeles*, is a musician especially well known for his slide guitar work. He first attracted public attention in the 1960s *when he played with Captain Beefheart and the Magic Band*.

In recent years, Cooder, *who has worked mainly as a studio musician*, has composed many film soundtracks, *the best known of which is perhaps the one he wrote for 'Paris Texas'*. Cooder has also played an important role in the increased appreciation of traditional Cuban music, especially in connection with the *Buena Vista Social Club* recording, *of which he was the producer*. The recording, *which was a worldwide hit*, was made by Cuban musicians, *some of whom had not played for many years*. In 1999, a documentary film, *(which was) directed by Wim Wenders, and (which was) nominated for an Academy Award* was made about the musicians.

100

2 Central Station in the city centre
3 the road with trees along one side
4 the pedestrianised area between two big shopping centres
5 the sign under a very tall streetlight
6 with the grey door, on the right
7 small statue on the right of the front door
8 The woman living next door
9 something to eat and drink
10 This sentence is best left unchanged – we don't usually replace a non-defining relative clause with *have* as the main verb.

101

Example answers:
2 Luxembourg is the only country in Northern Europe with no coastline / which doesn't have a coastline.

3 Death Valley in California, which was made (into) a National Park in 1994 and contains America's lowest point 86m below sea level, covers over 13,000 square kilometres.
4 The Amazon River Basin, which has more than 1000 tributaries / with more than 1000 tributaries, comprising over half of Brazil's land area, is the dominant geographical feature of the country.
5 India, bordered in / to the north by the Himalaya mountain range, dominated by vast river systems and plateaus further south, is a country with / which has extraordinary natural features and a rich cultural history.
6 Beijing, lying on a plain in north eastern China, has been a capital city since 1421.

102A

1 Both are possible, but the first is ambiguous – it could be the researchers, rather than the brushes, who have bristles.
2 that is (*that is* should be used between commas to add more detail. *which is* could also be used but needs to be punctuated as a relative clause: *The bristles' secret is the nanotube, which is a tiny straw-like molecule just 30 billionths of a metre across.*)
3 namely

102B

2 published
3 known
4 including
5 dipped
6 picking
7 coated / dipped
8 being

102C

1 with
2 or
3 and / or (*and* refers to one person with different roles. *or* refers to two people with different roles.)

103

Suggested answers:
In the beginning, there was Dr Jana Verwoerd, (2) *director of the Institute of Carbon Studies, who raised my interest in the topic.* She first showed me how carbon, (3) *this wonderful ancient substance, could be used in ways we had only dreamed of.* Then (4) *my close friend and mentor* Jamie Fussell gave me contacts in the world of industry, and several of his students helped to keep my enthusiasm for nanotechnology alive and burning. And of course Dr Katya Bubskya, (5) *one of the world's leading authorities in the field,* encouraged me to publish my work to the world.

But my greatest thanks are reserved for (6) *my dear wife and colleague*, Anna, without whom none of this would have been possible.

Thank you from the bottom of my heart.

104

(Corrections are given in italics.)
2 *Seeing / Witnessing the two people laughing and crying at the same time*, passers-by were moved by this emotional reunion between Jorge and Maria. (This has been amended because in the original sentence it is not clear whether it is the twins or the passers-by who are laughing and crying.)
3 Having been separated in their early teens, *the twins had been brought up by foster families* in different parts of the country.
(This has been amended because the original sentence means that the foster families (rather than the twins) were separated in their early teens.)
4 *Not wishing to upset the children, / Wishing not to upset the children,* neither foster family had spoken about the other twin.
5 ✓
6 *After leaving school*, she went to university... / Having left school, she went to university... / On leaving school, she went to university...
(The original sentence suggests that she went to university at exactly the same time as she left school, rather than some time after she had left school.)
7 *Having graduated / After graduating, she was taken on* by a large company as a management trainee.
(The subject of participle clauses like these must also be the subject of the main clause. In the original sentence, the implied subject of the participle clause is *Maria*, while the subject of the main clause is *a large company*.)
8 *Being unhappy in his new family*, Jorge ran away from home.
(This has been amended because in the original sentence, it is not clear that Jorge ran away from home because he was unhappy. The reason must come before the resulting action.)
9 *Stealing some money from a shop, / Having stolen some money from a shop, Jorge was arrested by the police* and went to prison for a year.
(The original sentence means that the police (rather than Jorge) had stolen money from a shop. Starting the sentence with *Having stolen* implies a delay between the two actions: stealing and being arrested. Starting the sentence with *Stealing* suggests that the police arrested Jorge in the act of stealing.)
10 ✓
11 Twenty years later, watching TV, he saw a programme about people looking for lost relatives, *and decided* to try to find his sister.

105A

2 Being more likely to arouse sympathy,... / More likely to arouse sympathy,...

3 Having been born with a deformed foot, she had been left... / Being born with a deformed foot, she had been left... / Born with a deformed foot, she had been left...

4 Wearing nothing on her feet, she went... (Note: *Having nothing on her feet...* would not be correct here because it would suggest the meaning 'because she had nothing on her feet...')

5 Reaching the age of twelve,... / Having reached the age of twelve,... / Aged twelve,...

6 Though getting / being paid very little,... / Despite getting / being paid very little,...

105B

2 Being the eldest (child) / As the eldest (child), she suffered most from her father's violent behaviour.

3 On one occasion, before coming home for / on her day off, she had visited / visited her aunt in Newcastle.

4 Having missed the last bus home, she stayed overnight in the city.

5 Having arrived home / On arriving home / Arriving home she was beaten by her stepfather / her stepfather beat her because he did not believe her story.
Or: Not believing her story, her stepfather beat her when she arrived home.

106

1 He saw a TV documentary about Australia.

2 Because they have *made sacrifices for him.* (This probably means they have spent money on him, perhaps on his education; they expect him to respect their wishes because of this.)

3 Nothing. He has decided to go, *whatever they say.*

4 To earn enough money to pay for his flight to Australia.

5 Probably not – he doesn't want to work more than he has to: *without having to work more than a couple of evenings a week.*

107

Example answers:

1 Not wishing to shock or upset anyone, I told nobody that I was getting married.

2 Having forgotten to tell anyone my new address, I shouldn't have been surprised when I didn't receive any birthday cards.

3 Since I left home, I have only spoken to my parents once every two or three weeks.

4 Before telling them my plans, I had asked my parents to buy me a car.

5 Unaware of my plans, my parents lent me quite a lot of money.

6 Without thinking about the problems that might occur, I bought myself an expensive car.

7 On arriving home that night, I received a frosty reception.

8 What with not getting on with my brother, I should have foreseen the jealousies that my car would provoke.

9 A little ashamed of what I had done, I told him he could borrow my car.

10 With the family being so short of money, it was the least I could do.

108A

1 b 2 e 3 c 4 h 5 a
6 f 7 g 8 d

108B

Suggested answers:

b in so doing (This is more formal than *in doing so.*)

c Laura did so

d more than me

e seemed likely to do this

f A bad break like this

g will when she can

h with a track record as impressive as hers / this

109

Example answer:

Art Chambers won the 110m hurdles at the last Olympic Games, and in so doing became the youngest man to break the 12-second barrier for the event. He won so easily that he seemed likely to do so again here, but it was not to be. He hit the first hurdle, and fell to the ground and broke his left arm. With such a disastrous start, he was never going to recover, and the race was won by his compatriot Allen Layne. His coach told waiting journalists that the accident would not put Art off coming back to compete at the highest levels, and he insists he will do so as soon as he is able.

110

1 not usually like this / not your usual self

2 Which one? / Which? (Using just *Which?* is quite informal.)

3 The silver ones. (Just *Silver* is also possible, but very informal.)

4 (All are possible.)

5 Which ones? / Which?

6 Those / Those ones

7 I imagine so / I imagine she has

8 (Both are possible.)

9 promised she would / promised to

10 I'm sure she will. / I expect so.

11 I doubt it / I doubt that he will

12 tear himself away

13 (All are possible, but *Yes it is* and *So it seems* imply that Laura already knew it was time to go, whereas *So it is* suggests she didn't.)

111

2 *To get themselves put in prison* emphasises that it was their own fault.

3 By using *Kaz and myself,* the speaker is suggesting that Kaz come too, but in a more diplomatic and less forceful way.

4 *little ones* = children; *loved ones* = family and friends who are close to you

5 The use of *one* and *oneself* to refer to people in general tells us that this is a formal context. In a less formal context you could replace with *you* and *yourself.*

6 No, because there is a direct object (*it*).

7 No, because *drag away* is a transitive verb which needs a direct object. In this case, as the subject and the object refer to the same person we use the reflexive pronoun *himself.*

8 *Didn't say so* means that he didn't say, and so we don't know. *Said not to* means he said don't take food and drink.

112

1 I am

2 I don't / I haven't / not

3 I would (be) / might (be)

4 I think so / (I think) I could / (I think) I'd be able to / I do

5 I did

6 I will

7 I do / have

8 there is

9 would

10 we do / I would

11 I am

113

2 We might be. / We might do. / We might.

3 Yes, I will (be).

4 ✓

5 I would, but I can't afford to / afford it.

6 I didn't think they would offer me the job, but they did / have.

7 ✓

8 Yes, I do. / Yes, I think you have. / Yes, I think you do. / Yes, I think so.

9 ✓ (*I thought it would be* is also possible.)

114

1 opportunity (to)

2 determined (to)

3 willing (to)

4 idea (to)

5 delighted (to)

6 plans (to)

7 want to

8 used to

9 'd (would) like (to) / want (to)

10 mean to

115

1 the world's fastest-growing hotel chain

2 ✓

3 boutique shops provided on-site (*Provided* is usually found after the noun.)

4 those required by law

5 *Stolen personal possessions* is more natural.

6 ✓

7 towels used (= towels that have been used; *used towels* = second-hand towels)

8 ✓

9 hair-raising ride

10 Those remaining / Those who remained

11 ✓

12 long-suffering guest

116

2 to sue
3 (that) they had
4 (that) they hadn't provided / they couldn't provide / they didn't provide
5 (about) admitting
6 to see
7 holding
8 (that) it was getting
9 what was happening / what was going to happen / what had happened
10 to go on / going on
11 to be told / that we were told
12 (of them) not to check (that) / not to have checked (that)
13 (about) asking / that we've asked

117

1 complete
2 pure / complete
3 similar (but not *alike*)
4 alike / similar
5 rash
6 chemical
7 tough
8 minimum
9 sheer
10 quick
11 afraid
12 alone

118

Suggested answers:
2 I was often a lone operator but I liked it that way.
3 I'd prefer to be remembered as a pretty good journalist than an absolutely perfect one.
4 Going to those places was dangerous, but I wanted to.
5 As I got older, I made a conscious decision to go on safer trips.
6 Knowing my husband was in the danger zone made me nervous.

119

2 ✓ the only solution possible / one possible solution
   ✗ one solution possible
3 (Both are possible, but with different meanings: *concerned people* = worried people, and *the people concerned* = the people who are affected.)
4 ✓ almost unheard of / rather unpopular
   ✗ very unheard of
5 ✓ very good / really wonderful
   ✗ very wonderful
6 ✓ almost unique / rather unusual
   ✗ utterly unusual
7 ✓ hugely disappointing / simply awful
   ✗ totally disappointing
8 (All are possible.)
9 ✓ perfectly lovely
   ✗ very lovely
10 ✓ maximum light
   ✗ the light to be maximum

120A

(Note: The difference in meaning is dependent on whether the adjective is gradable (you can put words like *very* in front of it) or non-gradable (a particular quality you can't have more or less of). *Very* can only go in front of the gradable adjectives.)
1a Wild animals (*wild* = not tamed)
1b a (very) wild social life (*wild* = uncontrolled)
2a public opinion (*public* = of the people)
2b a (very) public life (*public* = known about my most people)
3a (very) odd behaviour (*odd* = strange)
3b odd socks (*odd* = not matching)
4a French bread (*French* = from France)
4b a (very) French habit (*French* = typical of France)
5a a (very) adult way (*adult* = mature)
5b adult population (*adult* = over the age of 18)
6a Many (very) old people (*old* = not young)
6b old boyfriend or girlfriend (*old* = previous)

120B

Example answers:
A critical mass of votes is required to make elections valid (non-gradable; *critical* = a fixed necessary number or amount)
People who are very critical of others quickly become unpopular. (gradable; *critical* = making judgements)

The average person just wants to lead a law-abiding life. (non-gradable; *average* = typical of most people)
Most modern music is pretty average. (gradable; *average* = poor)

You can trust most antique sellers to sell you the genuine article (non-gradable; *genuine* = real)
Most film stars don't seem to be very genuine people. (gradable; *genuine* = honest)

121

2 In the mid-1970s, academics thought they had discovered why boys were not as good at reading as girls.
3 Apparently, boys tend to socialise later than girls, who are not as inclined to introspective activities.
4 Girls, on the other hand, are less interested in doing something creative.
5 Boys also tend not to read as quickly as girls.
6 Parents are more concerned about this phenomenon than educationalists.
7 Some researchers believe that boys' methodical approach to a text explains why they prefer non-fiction, as their mentality is less well-suited to understanding feelings than information.

122

1 It was OK, but it wasn't quite as comfortable a hotel as we'd expected.
2 In fact, one day it was absolutely blistering – much too hot / too hot for us.
3 Most of the time it was so overcooked that it was inedible.
4 ✓
5 At least it wasn't as expensive as the theatre.
6 Yes, but he just didn't play as well / well enough, did he?
7 No, Ruddock was certainly the best player on the day.
8 The truth is that Henstock is not such a good player / not as good a player as Ruddock.
9 I didn't think I'd enjoy the food at that restaurant, but I couldn't have been more wrong.
10 It was the tastiest fish that I've ever eaten.
11 ✓
12 How high a grade did you need to get?

123

1 Sentence a = The clothes are very unusual, not just for her but for anyone.
  Sentence b = These clothes are more unusual than other clothes she wears for work.
2 This set of sentences has a similar meaning. Sentence b is the only one which implies that she is not clever.
3 This set of sentences has a similar meaning.
4 This set of sentences has a similar meaning.
5 This set of sentences has a similar meaning, but the use of *sufficiently* makes sentence b more formal.
6 This set of sentences has a similar meaning but sentence a puts the greatest emphasis on Maria's achievement.
7 This set of sentences has a similar meaning, but the use of *even more* with *cold* emphasises the comparison between this winter and last.

124

(Alternative positions are shown in italics.)
2 Tim Appleyard, who was delayed by an overdue bus, (*angrily*) walked (*angrily*) out of school <u>angrily</u> after being given a detention for his late arrival.
3 The boy is refusing to accept his punishment even though (*eventually*) this may <u>eventually</u> lead (*eventually*) to his exclusion from the school (*eventually*).
4 <u>This morning</u> the headteacher of the school in an interview (*this morning*) said (*this morning*) that the boy only had himself to blame.
5 He said it was the responsibility of all students to ensure they arrived (*on time*) at school <u>on time</u>...
6 ...and he stressed that the boy should have caught an earlier bus to make sure he arrived <u>promptly</u>. (No other position is possible.)
7 The boy's parents have <u>severely</u> criticised the school (*severely*) for their rigidity.
8 His mother said <u>furiously</u>... (No other position is possible.)
9 'We are <u>completely</u> amazed by the school's inflexible attitude.' (No other position is possible.)
10 'Staff <u>really</u> should (*really*) spend more time on important issues like teaching.'
11 'He has never (*deliberately*) missed school <u>deliberately</u>.'

125

1. really (*Real* could be used here in informal American English.)
2. deeply = very much
3. unexpectedly
4. just = a very short time ago
5. flatly = completely
6. quickly
7. short (*to stop short (of doing)* = to nearly do something)
8. wide = completely, fully
9. lately = recently
10. directly = as soon as, very soon after
11. high = a long way up

126

1. Motorists who drive illegally are being caught and fined ▲ thanks to the introduction of new number plate readers. (automatically)
2. Traffic police are ▲ to check computer records ▲. (regularly)
   (In the final position in this sentence, *regularly* refers directly to the checking of computer records, rather than the regular use of readers. To *regularly check* is also possible, but some people avoid 'splitting the infinitive' in this way.)
3. They ▲ let officers know ▲ whether vehicles are taxed and insured, or whether drivers are wanted for other offences. (immediately)
4. Since the technology was introduced ▲ the team have made more than 1,000 arrests for driving and criminal offences. (three years ago)
5. The police inspector who ▲ leads the project, said... (currently)
6. 'Untaxed vehicles, road safety offences and crime are ▲ linked.' (clearly)
7. 'Our new system seems to be working ▲ as a way of catching people who shouldn't be on our roads.' (very efficiently)

127

(Alternative positions are shown in italics.)
1. The first and only time we met was (*on a cold November night in an upstairs bar*). / The first and only time we met was (*in an upstairs bar on a cold November night*).
2. ✓ Also possible: (*Excitedly*) I'd answered the ad / I'd (*excitedly*) answered the ad
3. There was a simple quality to her writing that had (*greatly*) appealed to me / that had appealed (*greatly*) to me / that had appealed to me (*greatly*).
4. ✓
5. I decided straightaway that I (*definitely*) wanted to see her again.
6. ✓
7. If only I could (*successfully*) manage the rest of the evening / If only I could manage the rest of the evening (*successfully*)
8. ✓ Also possible: Once ready, she stood there, waiting for me (*patiently*). Once ready, she stood there, waiting (*patiently*) for me.

9. (*firmly*) gripping the collar with my left hand / gripping the collar (*firmly*) with my left hand
10. I stretched my left arm (*backwards*) to catch the left sleeve.
11. ✓
12. (*Completely*) absorbed in what I was doing
13. I didn't notice that my body was beginning to move (*in an undignified way / fashion*) in an anti-clockwise direction.
14. ✓
15. the sleeve remained (*stubbornly*) the same distance from my hand.
16. ✓ Also possible: It was as if the sleeves had grown (*closer*) together while we'd been in the bar.
17. I grunted and groaned (*loudly*) as I struggled
18. or more (*accurately*) perhaps, the upper sleeve.
19. ✓ Also possible: twisting and stabbing (*madly*)
20. a (*fast-moving*) sleeve
21. ✓ Also possible: I sank (*slowly*) to the ground.
22. Lying there in a heap with my coat (*partially*) covering me...
23. ✓ Also possible: Never before had she seen a man (*so aggressively*) wrestled to the ground / Never before had she seen a man wrestled to the ground (*so aggressively*) by his own coat.

128

1. too
2. before
3. to Madrid leave hourly
4. much / very much
5. much
6. almost always looks tired
7. very
8. he alone
9. before / until
10. did I realise (*I realised* is also possible but less likely.)

129

1. a = Simon feeds the birds but no other animals.
   b = Simon but no one else feeds the birds.
   c = Simon feeds the birds in the winter but at no other time of the year.
   d = The same basic meaning as sentence c, but by starting the sentence with *Only in winter*, the writer is emphasising this fact.
2. a = It was not her usual custom to be early.
   b = She is sometimes early but this time she was earlier than usual.
3. a = The writer's belief is sincere.
   b = The writer believes that the other person was being sincere.
4. a = Two changes are taking place at the same time: the sun going down and the temperature dropping.
   b = This suggests that the drop in temperature may happen after the sun goes down.
5. These three sentences all have the same meaning.

130

Answer: The man lived in New York. His wife saw him off from New York in the morning and greeted him on his return in the evening.

1. ▲, a businessman had an important meeting that involved his flying from London to New York. / A businessman had an important meeting ▲ that involved his flying from London to New York. / A businessman had an important meeting that involved flying from London to New York ▲. (one day last week)
2. When he left home in the morning, his wife drove him ▲ and accompanied him to the check-in. (to the airport)
3. ▲ (Then), she waved him goodbye ▲ (as) he went through Passport Control. (then / as)
4. She did some shopping ▲ and returned to the car. (at the airport shops)
5. ▲ she was getting into her car, her husband's plane was taking off. / She was getting into her car ▲ her husband's plane was taking off. (as)
6. ▲, his flight from London to New York was direct. / His flight from London to New York was ▲ direct. / His flight from London to New York was direct, ▲. (naturally)
7. ▲ he reached New York, he went directly through Immigration and Customs. (when)
8. He had no baggage to collect as he had taken ▲ a briefcase for his short trip. / He had no baggage to collect as he had ▲ taken a briefcase for his short trip. (only)
9. He went through to the Arrivals Hall and ▲ his wife was there to greet him. (incredibly)
10. It was ▲ that morning that she had seen him off. (only)
11. ▲ had she travelled by plane or boarded a ship. (at no time during the day)
12. The question is this: how could the man's wife have met him ▲? (at the airport)

131A

1. one morning
2. from outside their house
3. promptly
4. Later the same day
5. from work
6. neatly
7. very
8. urgently
9. the following weekend / the next weekend
10. too / very
11. gratefully
12. The next weekend / The following weekend
13. when
14. Astonishingly

131B

Example answer:
One morning a young couple woke up to find that their car had been stolen from outside their house (*no change*). (Promptly), they phoned the police (promptly) and reported the theft. They returned home later the same day to find the car back again in the usual place.

There was also an envelope placed neatly under the windscreen wiper. Inside was a very (*no change*) polite note of apology. The writer explained that he had borrowed the car because his wife was having a baby and he'd had to take her urgently to the hospital. To make up for this, there were also two free tickets to a big rock concert the following weekend (*no change*). The young couple weren't too (*no change*) angry and gratefully accepted the tickets.

132
2 so (that)
3 seeing as
4 While / Though
5 so (that)
6 so as not to
7 to
8 though
9 With

133
Suggested answers:
2 Though
3 so that we can / to
4 Because / As
5 Though I'm convinced / Though I'm sure
6 so (that)
7 because / as

134
2 We worked on two sites and two computer networks so that there was no risk of losing any data. / So that there was not risk of losing any data, we worked on two sites and two computer networks.
3 In spite of two valuable team members leaving mid-way through, we managed to meet our deadlines. / We managed to meet our deadlines in spite of two valuable members leaving mid-way through.
4 Exhausted though we were / Though we were exhausted, the final two months were the most productive of all! / The final two months were the most productive of all, though we were exhausted!
5 It was due to the hard work of the whole team that we succeeded. / Our success was due to the hard work of the whole team.

135
2 The success of the experiment was + b (largely *due to / owing to* careful preparation).
3 We wondered if the colour had changed because + g (*of the presence of a gas*).
4 *Owing to / Due to* the massive weight of the material, + c (it proved impossible to construct strong enough equipment to measure it accurately).
5 Difficult *though* the conditions were, + d (we managed to retrieve over 50 samples).
6 The plants were all the healthier + e (*for* exposure to fresh air and sunlight).
7 It was such a minute particle to detect + a (*that* equipment had to be extremely precise).
8 *Because* this method hadn't been tried before, + f (we were unsure how the results would come out).

136A
1 while
2 inasmuch as (The other options are not possible as clarification is required here, rather than contrast.)
3 whereas / while
4 so as to / in order to
5 while / whereas
6 so that (introduces an explanation) / because (introduces a reason)
7 in such a way that / so that

136B
2 Despite the fact that they repeated
3 so (that) they could see
4 Primitive though the technology was / (Al)though the technology was primitive
5 even if / when (= whether or not)
6 Even though (= despite the fact that)
7 While intending / While they intended
8 such that / in such a way that

137
1 think
2 will / would
3 were
4 I'd
5 win
6 haven't won
7 I'm going to stop / I'll stop
8 whether
9 if you don't / unless you
10 as if
11 *will work* is the most likely answer as speaker B is making a strong point or seems critical of speaker A.
12 was / were
13 unless you'd
14 if it were / were it (*were it* is very formal.)
15 makes / will make
16 whether
17 happen / should happen
18 if / whether
19 means

138
1 If I might
2 Were it not for
3 Should
4 Had we not
5 we would undoubtedly
6 whether or not
7 If you were
8 I would
9 unless
10 If that were to happen
11 we would
12 Imagine
13 could

139A
1 b
2 a
3 d
4 c

139B
Suggested answers:
1 ...global warming will become a more serious problem.
2 What alternative energy sources would we use?
3 ...we wouldn't need so much oil.
4 This might solve all our energy problems.
5 ...it should still be taken seriously.
6 ...the countries of the world cooperate.
7 ...people would be forced to use alternative methods of transport.
8 ...there would still be plentiful supplies of oil left.

140
1 though
2 though
3 so
4 so
5 though
6 Suggested answers: much / badly
7 Suggested answer: upset

141
2 as well / too
3 Before that
4 So long as (*Provided that* is too formal for this context.)
5 unless
6 Anyway / In any case

142
1
People have dragged heavy objects, such as the bodies of hunted animals, along the ground from the beginning of human history. (a) *Before long*, early humans realised that using 'runners' made from smooth wood made dragging much easier, especially over snow and ice, and the sledge had been invented. (b) *At the same time*, hunting techniques improved, and human communities started to prosper.

2
The first wheels to be invented were heavy, being made of solid wood, (b) *and hence* the invention of wheels with spokes, which were lighter and allowed much faster travel. (c) *Even so*, early carts could only travel at three or four kilometres per hour. (a) *However*, they allowed people and animals to move much greater weights more efficiently than before.

3
Roman roads required enormous quantities of material, and a huge workforce, to complete. (c) *In addition*, they went forward in almost straight lines, and had very steep sections up and down hills. (a) *As a result*, individual Roman soldiers did not always praise the engineers as they toiled up a hillside. (b) *Nevertheless*, the new roads enabled soldiers to travel quickly over long distances, and many of the roads were so well made that they lasted hundreds or even thousands of years.

143

Example answers:
2 ...this one is surprisingly economical.
3 ...I'm going to make something to eat.
4 ...I'll have to put those on the back seat.
5 ...you had to take a train and then a slow bus service.
6 ...I don't know my way around here.
7 ...I enjoyed the meal.
8 ...shall we go for a walk...
9 ...we are members of her family.

144

1 among
2 along (Here *along with* means *together with* or *in addition to*.)
3 across (= we are thinking of the lobby here as a surface (floor area) to be crossed) / through (= we are thinking of the lobby as a three-dimensional area, maybe busy with people and luggage)
4 over (= covering a wide area) / across (= suggests the movement of a large number of jewels on the surface of the lobby)
5 across / through (The same distinction as in item 3 above.)
6 Between

145

(Answer: The woman juggled the balls as she went across the bridge.)
1 through
2 along
3 over / across
4 ✓
5 across / over
6 over / across

146

1 along
2 through
3 along
4 across / through
5 under / below
6 over
7 across
8 between
9 between
10 Between
11 among
12 between
13 among

147

1 an experienced politician
2 a helicopter
3 someone with flu
4 someone watching a horror film
5 someone who has lost their door key
6 people with sensitive or secret information
7 a doctor
8 a prisoner escaping from a high security jail
9 a university graduate

148

Example answers:
1 Where's the cat hiding?
2 Where do people play football?
3 How did he react when he heard the news?
4 What's the matter with your sister?
5 Where did the tennis ball hit him?
6 Where can you spend US dollars?
7 Where do you find submarines?
8 Where do planes fly?

149

2 No direct replacement is possible, but you could say *up to / till now* instead of *so far today*.
3 during / within
4 apart from / with the exception of
5 up to, up till. (*till* is also possible, but a little informal for a radio news programme.)
6 Over, During
7 Besides (*Except for* is less likely at the start of a sentence in a short clause.)
8 during, in
9 up till / until (*till* is also possible, but a little informal for a radio news programme.)
10 in, during, for
11 During / In (*During* and *In* are possible alternatives, although *Throughout* emphasises that the scoreline stayed the same for most of the first half.)
12 so far / up to now / up till now
13 In addition to / As well as
14 (There is no real equivalent to *by* which has the meaning 'at the end of the year or before'.)

150

2 aside
3 During (= at some time but not necessarily all the time) / Throughout (= all the time I was in Malaysia)
4 During
5 but
6 except (that)
7 apart from
8 Except for / Apart from
9 up till
10 so far
11 by

151

Example answers:
1 I was working in an office until a year ago, but I left to go travelling.
2 I found it very difficult to cope with the different culture during my first job abroad.
3 I'd been studying for a PhD up to the end of last year, and it was a very big change to go from that to working.
4 I'd like to be running my own business by the time I'm 40.
5 I think I've enjoyed almost everything, except perhaps my final exams at university – they were really stressful.
6 I've been to most parts of the world, except for South America – I'd love to visit Peru one day.

152

2 d framed within the camera's eye (*within* has a similar meaning to *in*, but has an extra sense of 'enclosed by')
3 i waiting for what he called
4 f Inspired by other photographers' images
5 c equipped with a then-revolutionary lightweight
6 e influenced by surrealism
7 a became friends with
8 g reveal the beauty within / of
9 b collaborated with several filmmakers (*collaborate with* other people; *collaborate on* projects or activities)
10 j went on working until (*went on* = continued)

153

1 improvements in
2 be proud of
3 determination to succeed
4 desire to do
5 chance of attaining / chance to attain
6 amazement at
7 lack of
8 improvement in
9 prospect of
10 failure to make
11 possibility of having to
12 satisfied with

154

1 a
2 b
3 to deal / of dealing (*way* = method)
4 of dealing (*way* = manner)
Sentences 6 and 7 suggest Jane was not present.
8 b (*agree with* suggests a shared opinion)
9 a

155

2 agree to / talk about
3 interview with
4 talk on / talk about
5 involved in
6 discussion on / of / about
7 proposals to
8 sole intention of
9 option of
10 permission to

156

2 to + b
3 to + a
4 of + d
5 to + g
6 of + f
7 of + c

157

2 sort out the party arrangements
3 take you up on your offer
4 hear me out
5 ran into her
6 call me back
7 help me off with
8 talk my brother out of

9 take over one of his business rivals / take one of his business rivals over
10 go over it
11 come in for a lot of criticism
12 look up to him
13 cleaning up the garage / cleaning the garage up
14 thrown away lots of things / thrown lots of things away

158

1 turn up (transitive) = increase the volume
turned up (intransitive) = came (to see something)
2 hold out (intransitive) = continue to resist / not give in
hold out (transitive) = put or stretch forward
3 split up (intransitive) = separate / stop being a couple
splits (the class) up (transitive) = divide / arrange in different groups
4 broke in (intransitive) = entered by force
break in (transitive) = train someone / help someone get used to a new job or position
5 cut out (intransitive) = stopped working
cut it out (transitive) = remove using knife or scissors
6 picked it up (transitive) = caught (a disease)
picked up (intransitive) = improved / became more interesting or fast moving
7 look up (intransitive) = look in an upward direction
look it up (transitive) = search for information about (e.g. in a dictionary / encyclopaedia)
8 look it out (transitive) = find (perhaps with difficulty)
Look out! (intransitive) = Be careful! / Watch out!

159

(Errors are underlined and numbered below. Corrections are given separately.)

(1) There <u>were</u> a door to the left and another to the right, and she went through the one on the left. Her eyes started to become accustomed to the darkness, and (2) <u>she noticed it how she felt cold</u> in this room with high ceilings. (3) <u>There were dust in the air</u>, lit up by sunlight coming through a thin gap between the curtains. There was dark, heavy furniture in the room, and (4) <u>there was tall bookcases</u> which stood all along one wall. (5) <u>There were an old-fashioned sofa and two chairs</u> in one corner, but (6) <u>she was most surprised by there were</u> clocks everywhere, on every surface – there was even one or two on the arms of chairs – and it was clear none of them worked.
Corrections:
(1) was
(2) she noticed how she felt cold / she noticed how cold she felt (We don't use *it* as the object of *notice*.)
(3) There was dust in the air
(4) there were tall bookcases
(5) There was an old-fashioned sofa and two chairs
(6) but what surprised her most was that there were

160

Example answers:
2 what we were asked to do was write about foreign policy
3 What I said was (that) I would try to come but I wasn't sure.
4 What upsets me / What's upsetting me is / what upset me was that he won't commit to a relationship - and we've been together for nearly two years now.
5 what I decided to do was see them separately on different nights.

161

Suggested answers:
2 it amazed me to hear
3 The shirt's
4 leave it to me to do (Note: *leave it to me*, a common expression, is also possible.)
5 it struck me (*Strike* very commonly has the meaning *occur to* or make *(somebody) think*.)
6 I can't guarantee (it) that (*Guarantee* is more common without *it*.) (Note: *It can't be guaranteed* is also possible.)
7 it transpired that it was taken (*transpire* = emerged / turn out)

162

2 it was Jon who
3 when you tell lies
4 What started it was
5 there's no need
6 what he said was
7 What I suggest
8 there's a film and a football match

163

2 The original text has *it strikes me that* but *it occurs to me* would also be possible.
3 Is there a
4 It's a bit difficult to
5 It emerges (= becomes apparent)
6 there were
7 What I used to do (The *what-* clause allows the speaker to leave the important information to the end for impact.)
8 It is said that
9 It's an
10 it occurs to me
11 there is
12 it's all

164

1 Hardly
2 Had
3 Such
4 So
5 Should
6 Little
7 Had it not been

165

1 It may seem fast to you, but at no time since we left home have I broken the speed limit.
2 Here comes a police car!
3 ✓

4 I kept waiting, then along came three at the same time.
5 She's much quicker than I am at finding information.
6 ✓ (*than are their parents* is also possible.)
7 There goes my lunch!
8 ✓
9 There goes the phone.

166

1 Not until
2 neither do
3 in walked
4 off he went
5 No sooner
6 Little do they

167

2 ...as were the Italian people.
3 ...not once did we have pizza.
4 Several times while we were there we had pasta... / Several times we had pasta while we were there...
5 ...neither did Polly.
6 At no time did we feel bored or at a loose end.
7 had I known we were going to enjoy our stay so much,...

168

Your own ideas. Use the email in exercise 67 as a model.